Destiny, Freedom,
and the Soul

Destiny, Freedom, *and the* Soul

What Is the Meaning of Life?

Osho

St. Martin's Griffin
New York

Contents

Destiny, Freedom,
and the Soul

Introduction

Man is a quest—not a question, but a quest. A question can be solved intellectually, but a quest must be solved existentially. It is not that we are seeking some answers to some questions; it is that we are seeking some answer to our being.

It is a quest, because questions are about others. A quest is about oneself. Man is seeking himself. He knows he *is*, but he does not know *who* he is. Hence, a great inquiry arises in the innermost core of every human being at the moment of birth. We can suppress that inquiry, we can divert that inquiry, we can change that inquiry for substitute inquiries, but we cannot kill it. There is no way to kill it, because it is intrinsic to human nature. It is intrinsic to consciousness to know one's quest.

That inquiry is our very nature, and unless it is resolved, we remain searching. Of course, there are 999 ways to go wrong, and there is only one way to go right—so the search is full of hazards. The quest is not simple; it is very complex—and it is very rare that a person achieves resolution. But unless you reach for it, you will continue in agony, in turmoil. You will remain a cry in the wilderness. You will not know what joy is. Not knowing yourself, how can you be joyous? And you will not know what benediction is. Not knowing yourself, there is no benediction.

You will hear words like *contentment* and *blissfulness,* but they will remain words. They won't have any meaning for you. The meaning has to be supplied by your experience. They will remain empty words, they will create much noise around you, but they will not signify anything.

Search is intrinsic to human nature. But then arises the problem that there are many ways to go wrong. How to find the right path?

Thomas Carlyle said, "The misfortune of man has its source in his greatness. For there is something infinite in him and he cannot succeed in burying himself completely in the finite."

There is something in you that is higher than you, bigger than you, and there is no way to bury it somewhere in the finite. You can see it in your own life. You can seek money and power, but each time you succeed, you will find that you have failed. Each time you succeed, the success will bring nothing but the awareness of your failure. Money is there, but you are as dissatisfied as ever, or even more so. Power is there and you are as impotent as ever. Nothing makes one more aware of powerlessness than power. Nothing makes one more aware of inner poverty than riches—because of the contrast. You can see that there are riches outside, but inside, you are a beggar, still desiring and asking and hankering and searching.

From one side, this seems to be a misfortune—the misery of man. From another side, it is his greatness. Carlyle was right when he said that the misfortune of man has its source in his greatness.

What is this greatness? This greatness is the human capacity to surpass oneself, to go beyond oneself, to make a ladder of one's life, to jump out of oneself. Unless that jump has happened, you live in a wasteland; nothing will ever bloom there. You can make all the efforts possible, but the desert will remain a desert; you will not come across any flowers.

Those flowers start blooming only when you have started reaching somewhere close to truth. That is the quest. The quest is that the human being longs to become God. The quest is that the human being wants to become truth. You want to feel it—that "I am truth." Nothing less than that will ever satisfy you.

The Mystery of "Who Am I?"

"Who am I?" has to be asked in the deepest recesses of your being. You have to resound with this question. It has to vibrate in you, pulsate in your blood, in your cells. It has to become a question mark in your very soul.

And when the mind is silent, you will know. Not that some answer will be received by you in words, not that you will be able to write it down in your notebook that "This is the answer." Not that you will be able to tell anybody, "This is the answer." If you can tell anybody, it is not the answer. If you can write it down in a notebook, it is not the answer. When the real answer comes to you, it is so existential that it is inexpressible.

I myself am a question. I know not who I am.
What to do? Where to go?

Remain with the question. Don't do anything, and don't go anywhere; and don't start believing in any answer. Remain with the question.

That is one of the most difficult things to do—to remain with a question and not to seek the answer. Because the mind is very cunning, it can supply a false answer. It can console you; it can give you something to cling to; and then the question is not answered but suppressed. Then you go on believing in the answer, and the question remains deep down in your unconsciousness like a wound. The healing has not happened.

If you remain with the question, I'm not saying that you will receive the answer. Nobody has ever received any answer. If you remain with the question, by and by the question disappears. Not because the answer is received; there is no answer. There cannot be, because life is a mystery. If there is any answer, then life will not be a mystery.

It has no answer to it; it cannot be solved. It is not a puzzle; it is a mystery. And that is the difference between a puzzle and a mystery. A puzzle can be solved, howsoever difficult it is to solve. A mystery cannot be solved—not that it is difficult. It is very simple, but its nature is such that it cannot be solved.

Remain with the question—alert, aware, not seeking, not trying to find an answer. Very arduous it is, but if you can do that . . . it can be done. I have done it. And all those who have dissolved their questions have done it. The very awareness, the fire of awareness, burns the question. The sun of awareness melts the question; it disappears, it evaporates. One day, suddenly, you find you are there, and the question is not there. Not that the question is replaced by an answer. There is none. But the question has simply disappeared. You are there and without a question. That is the answer.

You, without a question, is the answer. Not that you will be able to say who you are—you will laugh at the very question. The question has become absurd. In the first place, the very asking was wrong. But right now, you cannot understand that; you have to ask. You have to ask very intensely. Ask the question, but don't ask for the answer.

That is the difference between theology and religiousness. Theology gives you the answer; religiousness gives you awareness. Theology supplies you answers—ready-made, manufactured, polished, perfect. Religiousness doesn't give you any answer; it simply helps you to penetrate deep into the question. The deeper you go into the question, the more you find it is melting, it is disappearing. And when the question has disappeared, a tremendous energy is released within you. You are there, with no question.

And when there is no question, of course, there is no mind. Mind is the questioner. When there is no questioning, the mind has also disappeared—pure consciousness—just the sky without any clouds, the flame without any smoke.

That's what godliness is. That's what a Buddha is; that's what a Christ is. Remember, I repeat it again and again: Buddha has not found the answer; that's why Buddha never answers the most essential questions. You ask him, "Does God exist?" He will avoid the question; he will not answer. You ask him, "What happens when a person dies?" He will avoid it; he will start talking about other things. He will not answer.

He is not a metaphysician, and he is not a philosopher. He has come to face the question, and the question has disappeared. The question disappears as darkness disappears when you kindle a light, when you bring a lamp. Bring more awareness to the question.

You say, "I myself am a question." Beautiful! That's how it should be—reduce all questions to the basic question, and that is,

"Who am I?" Don't go on moving around the periphery with questions like "Who made the world? Why was the world created?" Those are all nonsense questions. Come to the basic question, the most fundamental question: Who am I?

Who? Let your consciousness penetrate into it, like a deep arrow going deeper and deeper and deeper. And don't be in a hurry to find the answer—because the mind is cunning. If you are in a hurry, impatient, the mind can supply you with an answer. The mind can quote scriptures; it is the devil! It can say, "Yes, you are a god, you are pure consciousness, you are the ultimate truth, an eternal soul, a deathless being." Those answers can destroy your very search.

A seeker has to be aware of ready-made answers. They are available; from every side they are being supplied to you. In fact, your mind has already been conditioned. The answers have been given to you before you even asked the question.

A small child—he has not asked who God is, and he is being supplied with the answer; he is being conditioned. He has not asked—the question is still not there, and already the answer is being given. Many people go on believing in these answers throughout their lives, and they never ask the question themselves.

If you have not asked the question, whatever you know is just rubbish. Throw it on the rubbish heap, all your knowledge—because in reality, there is no knowledge, there is only knowing. There is no answer, only a state of consciousness where the questioning disappears. Only a clarity, a clarity of vision and perception, a clarity of eyes; you can see through and through—not that you find an answer somewhere.

Existence is so vast, so mysterious . . . and it is good that it is so. Just think of the misfortune if you could have found the answer. Then life would not be worth living; then it would not have any meaning. Because you cannot find the answer, life goes on having infinite meaning. God is not the answer; godliness is the state of being where the question has disappeared. Godliness is the state of no-mind.

Remain with the question. I am here to help you to remain with the question. I am not going to give you any answer; you already have too many. I am not going to burden you any more. I am to teach you how to unlearn the answers that you have learned, so that the question becomes crystal pure; so the question becomes authentic and yours; so the question arises from your innermost being.

And remain with it. Don't go here and there; don't be in a hurry. Be patient. Let this question become your constant companion.

This is the only discipline I teach: the discipline of questioning, and without being in any hurry for the answer.

And it is beautiful to remain with the question, because answers corrupt you. They destroy your innocence; they destroy your pure ignorance. They fill your mind with words, theories, dogmas; then you are no longer a virgin. They corrupt you. A question is pure; it does not corrupt you. In fact, it intensifies your purity; it makes you more and more clear.

Become aware of the question. Not that you have to continuously ask, "Who am I?" Not that you have to verbalize it. Let the question be there without any verbalization. Let it be like your breathing; let it be like your being. Let it be there, silent but continuous, as if you are pregnant with it. One day, if you have lived enough with the question, it starts disappearing. It evaporates, just as when the morning comes and the sun rises, and the dewdrops start disappearing. When the consciousness has become a fire, an intense light, the question starts disappearing.

And when the question has disappeared, you cannot say who you are, but you know. It is not knowledge; it is a *knowing*. You cannot answer, but you know. You can dance it; you cannot answer it. You can smile it; you cannot answer it. You will live it, but you cannot answer it.

Often I have the feeling that I am not doing something I ought to be doing, or doing something I should not be doing; that something has to change and fast—a schoolboy's worry that I am not going to make the grade, that I might be expelled.

This is how we all have been brought up. Our whole education—in the family, in the society, in the school, in the college, in the university—creates tension in us. And the fundamental tension is that you are not doing that which you ought to do.

Then it persists your whole life; it follows you like a nightmare, it goes on haunting you. It will never leave you at rest, it will never allow you to relax. If you relax, it will say, "What are you doing? You are not supposed to relax; you should be doing something." If you are doing something it will say, "What are you doing? You need some rest, it is a must, otherwise you will drive yourself crazy—you are already on the verge."

If you do something good, it will say, "You are a fool. Doing good is not going to pay—people will cheat you." If you do something bad, it will say, "What are you doing? You are preparing the way to go to hell, you will have to suffer for it." It will never leave you at rest; whatsoever you do, it will be there, condemning you.

This condemner has been implanted in you. This is the greatest calamity that has happened to humanity. And unless we get rid of this condemner inside us, we cannot be truly human, we cannot be truly joyous, and we cannot participate in the celebration that existence is.

And now nobody can drop it except you. And this is not only the questioner's problem, but this is also the problem of almost every human being. Whatever country you are born in, whatsoever religion you belong to, it doesn't matter—Catholic, communist, Hindu, Mohammedan, Jain, Buddhist, it does not matter to what kind of ideology you belong—the essential is the same. The essential is to create a split in you, so one part always condemns the other part. If you follow the first part, then the second part starts condemning you. You are in an inner conflict, a civil war.

This civil war has to be dropped; otherwise you will miss the whole beauty, the benediction of life. You will never be able to laugh to your heart's content, you will never be able to love, you will never be able to be total in anything. And it is only out of totality that one blooms, that the spring comes, and your life starts having color and music and poetry.

It is only out of totality that suddenly you feel the presence of godliness all around you. But the irony is that the split has been created by your so-called saints, priests, and churches. In fact, the priest has been the greatest enemy of real religiousness on the earth.

We have to get rid of all the priests; they are the root cause of human pathology. They have made everybody ill at ease; they have caused an epidemic of neuroses. And the neuroses have become so prevalent that we take them for granted. We think that this is all life is about, we think this is what life is—a suffering, a long, long, delayed suffering; a painful, agonizing existence; an autobiography of much ado about nothing.

And if we look at our so-called life, it seems so, because there is never a single flower, never a single song in the heart, never a ray of divine delight.

It is not surprising that intelligent people all over the world are asking what the meaning of life is. "Why should we go on living? Why are we so cowardly as to go on living? Why can't we gather a little courage and put a stop to all this nonsense? Why can't we commit suicide?"

Never before in the world have there been so many people thinking that life is so utterly meaningless. Why has this happened in this age? It has nothing to do with this age. For centuries, for at least five thousand years, the priests have been doing harm to the human psyche. Now it has reached the ultimate peak.

It is not our doing; we are victims. We are the victims of history. If man becomes a little more conscious, the first thing to be done is to burn all the history books. Forget the past—it was nightmarish. Start anew from *ABC*, as if Adam is born again. Start as if we are again in the Garden of Eden, innocent, uncontaminated, unpolluted by cruel priests and their ideas.

The priests have been very mean, because they discovered something tremendously significant for themselves: Divide a person, split a person, make him basically schizophrenic, and you will always remain in power. A divided human being is a weak human being. An undivided person, an individual, has strength—strength to accept any adventure, any challenge.

A man was looking for a good church to attend and found a small one in which the congregation was reading with the minister. They were saying, "We have left undone those things we ought to have done, and we have done those things which we ought not to have done."

The man dropped into a seat and sighed with relief as he said to himself, *Thank goodness, I've found my crowd at last.*

Go to any church, and you will find your crowd, you will find replicas of your being. Maybe the language is a little bit different, the ritual a little bit different, but the fundamentals are the same. The fundamental is that the human being has been reduced to an inner civil war.

The first day you recognize this, what the priests have done to you, is a day of great insight. And the day you drop all this nonsense is the day of the beginning of liberation.

Do what your nature wants to do. Do what your intrinsic qualities hanker to do. Don't listen to the scriptures. Listen to your own heart. That is the only scripture I prescribe. Yes, listen very attentively, very consciously, and you will never be wrong. And listening to your own heart, you will never be divided. Listening to your own heart, you will start moving in the right direction, without ever thinking of what is right and what is wrong.

So the whole art for the new humanity will consist in the secret of listening to the heart consciously, alertly, attentively. And follow it through any means, and go wherever it takes you. Yes, sometimes it will take you into dangers—but then remember, those dangers are needed to make you ripe. And sometimes it will take you astray—but remember again, those goings astray are part of growth. Many times you will fall. Rise up again, because this is how one gathers strength—by falling and rising again. This is how one becomes integrated.

But don't follow rules imposed from the outside. No imposed rule can ever be right, because rules are invented by people who want to rule you. Yes, sometimes there have been great enlightened people in the world, too—a Buddha, a Jesus, a Krishna, a Mohammed. They have not given rules to the world; they have given their love. But sooner or later the disciples gather together and start making codes of conduct. Once the master is gone, once the light is gone and they are in deep darkness, they start groping for certain rules to follow, because now the light in which they could have seen is there no more. Now they will have to depend on rules.

What Jesus did was his own heart's whispering, and what Christians go on doing is *not* their own hearts' whispering. They are imitators—and the moment you imitate, you insult your humanity, you insult your God.

Never be an imitator; be always original. Don't become a carbon copy. But that's what is happening all over the world—carbon copies and carbon copies.

Life is really a dance if you are an original—and you are meant to be an original. And no two people are alike, so my way of life can never become your way of life.

Listen to your own heart's whisperings—and they *are* whisperings. The heart speaks in a very still, small voice; it does not shout.

A Buddha is a Buddha, a Krishna is a Krishna, and you are you. And you are not in any way less than anybody else. Respect yourself, respect your own inner voice and follow it.

And remember, I am not guaranteeing that it will always lead you to the right. Many times it will take you to the wrong, because to come to the right door, one has to knock first on many wrong doors. That's how it is. If you suddenly stumble upon the right door, you will not be able to recognize that it is right.

In the ultimate reckoning, no effort is ever wasted. All efforts contribute to the ultimate climax of your growth. So don't be hesitant; don't be worried too much about going wrong. That is one of the problems; people have been taught never to do anything wrong, and then they become so hesitant, so fearful, so frightened of doing wrong, they become stuck. They cannot move—something wrong may happen. So they become like rocks: they lose all movement.

I teach you to commit as many mistakes as possible, remembering only one thing: Don't commit the same mistake again. And you will be growing. It is part of your freedom to go astray; it is part of your dignity to go even against God. And it is sometimes beautiful to go even against God. This is how you will start having a spine; otherwise, there are millions of people, spineless.

Because I say such things, many people are angered. Just the other day, a journalist came here. He had come to cover what is happening here in this place, and he wanted to have both stories—the people who are for it, and the people who are against it. So he went around the town. He talked to police officers; he went to see the mayor of Pune. And what the mayor said was really beautiful, I loved it.

He said, "This man is so dangerous that he should be expelled from Pune—not only from Pune but from India, not only from India but from the world!"

I loved it. And I started thinking about it. *Where will they expel me*

15

from the world? That's a really fantastic idea! If they can manage it, I am willing to go.

Why is there so much anger? The anger has a reason in it; it has a rationale behind it. The rationale is that I am trying to give you a totally new vision of religious life—and if the new vision succeeds, then all the old visions will have to die.

Forget all about what you have been told: "This is right and this is wrong." Life is not so fixed. The thing that is right today may be wrong tomorrow; the thing that is wrong this moment may be right the next moment. Life cannot be pigeonholed; you cannot label it so easily as, "This is right and this is wrong." Life is not a pharmacy, where every bottle is labeled and you know what is what. Life is a mystery; one moment something fits and then it is right. Another moment, so much water has gone down the Ganges that it no longer fits and it is wrong.

What is my definition of right? That which is harmonious with existence is right, and that which is disharmonious with existence is wrong. You will have to be very alert each moment, because it has to be decided each moment afresh. You cannot depend on ready-made answers for what is right and what is wrong. Only stupid people depend on ready-made answers, because then they need not be intelligent. There is no need: you already know what is right and what is wrong, you can cram the list, the list is not very big.

The Jews have Ten Commandments, so simple, you know what is right and what is wrong. But life goes on changing continuously. If Moses comes back, I don't think he will give you the same Ten Commandments—he cannot. After three thousand years, how can he give you the same commandments? He will have to invent something new.

But my own understanding is this, that whenever commandments are given, they create difficulties for people, because by the time they are given, they are already out of date. Life moves so fast; it is a dynamism, it is not static. It is not a stagnant pool, it is a Ganges, it goes on flowing. It is never the same for two consecutive moments. So one thing may be right this moment, and may not be right the next.

Then what to do? The only possible thing is to make people so aware that they themselves can decide how to respond to a changing life.

An old Zen story: There were two temples, rivals. Both the masters—they must have been so-called masters, must have really been priests—were so much against each other that they told their followers never to look at the other temple.

Each of the priests had a boy to serve him, to go and fetch things for him, to go on errands. The priest of the first temple told his boy servant, "Never talk to the other boy. Those people are dangerous."

But boys are boys. One day they met on the road, and the boy from the first temple asked the other, "Where are you going?"

The other said, "Wherever the wind takes me." He must have been listening to great Zen things in the temple; he said, "Wherever the wind takes me." A great statement, pure Tao.

But the first boy was very much embarrassed, offended, and he could not find how to answer him. Frustrated, angry, and also feeling guilty because, *My master said not to talk with these people. These*

people really are dangerous. Now, what kind of answer is this? He has humili-
ated me.

He went to his master and told him what had happened. "I am sorry that I talked to him. You were right: those people are strange. What kind of answer is this? I asked him, 'Where are you going?'—a simple formal question—and I knew he was going to the market, just as I was going to the market. But he said, 'Wherever the wind takes me.'"

The master said, "I warned you, but you didn't listen. Now look, tomorrow you stand at the same place again. When he comes ask him, 'Where are you going?' and he will say, 'Wherever the wind takes me.' Then you also be a little more philosophical. Say, 'If you don't have any legs, then? Because the soul is bodiless and the wind cannot take the soul anywhere!' What about that?"

Absolutely ready, the whole night he repeated it again and again and again. And next morning very early he went there, stood on the right spot, and at the exact time the boy came. He was very happy, now he was going to show him what real philosophy is. So he asked, "Where are you going?" And he was waiting....

But the boy said, "I am going to fetch vegetables from the market."

Now, what to do with the philosophy that he had learned?

Life is like that. You cannot prepare for it; you cannot be ready for it. That's its beauty, that's its wonder, that it always takes you unawares, it always comes as a surprise. If you have eyes, you will see that each moment is a surprise and no ready-made answer is ever applicable.

And all the old religions have supplied you with ready-made

answers. Manu has given his commandments, Moses has given his commandments, and so on and so forth.

I don't give you any commandment. In fact, the very word *commandment* is ugly. To command somebody is to reduce him to a slave. I don't give you any orders; you are not to be obedient to me or to anybody else. I simply teach you an intrinsic law of life. Be obedient to your own self, be a light unto yourself and follow the light, and this problem will never arise. Then whatsoever you do is the thing to do, and whatsoever you don't do is the thing that has not to be done.

And remember, don't go on looking back again and again, because life goes on changing. Tomorrow you may start thinking what you did yesterday was wrong. It was not wrong yesterday; it may look wrong tomorrow. There is no need to look back; life goes ahead. But there are many drivers who go on looking in the rearview mirror. They drive onward, but they look backwards; their life is going to be a catastrophe.

Look ahead. The road that you have passed, you have passed. It is finished; don't carry it anymore. Don't be unnecessarily burdened by the past. Go on closing the chapters that you have read; there is no need to go back again and again. And never judge anything of the past through the new perspective that is arriving, because the new is new, incomparably new. The old was right in its own context, and the new is right in its own context, and they are incomparable.

What I am trying to explain to you is this: Drop guilt! Because to be guilty is to live in hell. Not being guilty, you will have the freshness of dewdrops in the early morning sun, you will have the freshness of lotus petals in the lake, you will have the freshness of the stars in the night. Once guilt disappears, you will have a totally different kind of life, luminous and radiant. You will have a dance to your feet, and your heart will be singing a thousand and one songs.

To live in such rejoicing is to be a *sannyasin*, to live in such joy is to live a divine life. To live burdened with guilt is simply to be exploited by the priests.

Get out of your prisons—Hindu, Christian, Mohammedan, Jaina, Buddhist, communist. Get out of all your prisons, get out of all your ideologies, because ideologies supply you ready-made answers. If you ask the communist a question, he will have to look in *Das Kapital*. In the same way, if you ask the Hindu, he turns the pages of the Gita.

When are you going to use your own consciousness? When? How long are you going to remain tethered to the dead past? The Gita was born five thousand years back; life has changed so much. If you want to read the Gita, read it as beautiful literature—but just like that, no more than that. It is beautiful literature, it is beautiful poetry, but it has no dictums to be followed and no commandments to be followed. Enjoy it as a gift from the past, as the gift of a great poet, Vyasa. But don't make it a discipline for your life; it is utterly irrelevant.

And everything becomes irrelevant, because life never remains confined. It goes on and on; it crosses all borders, all boundaries, it is an infinite process. The Gita comes to a full stop somewhere, the Koran comes to a full stop somewhere, but life never comes to a full stop— remember that. Remind yourself of it.

And the only way to be in contact with life, the only way not to lag behind life, is to have a heart that is not guilty, a heart that is innocent. Forget all about what you have been told—what has to be done and what has not to be done—nobody else can decide it for you.

Avoid those pretenders who decide for you; take the reins in your own hands. You have to decide. In fact, in that very decisiveness, your soul is born. When others decide for you, your soul remains asleep and dull. When you start deciding on your own, a sharpness arises. To decide means to take risks, to decide means you may be doing wrong—who knows? That is the risk. Who knows what is going to happen? That is the risk—there is no guarantee.

With the old, there is a guarantee. Millions and millions of people have followed it—how can so many people be wrong? That is the guarantee. If so many people say it is right, it must be right.

In fact, the logic of life is just the opposite. If so many people are following a certain thing, be certain it is wrong, because so many people are not so enlightened and cannot be so enlightened. The majority consists of fools, utter fools. Beware of the majority. If so many people are following something, that is enough proof that it is wrong.

Truth happens to individuals, not to crowds. Have you ever heard of a crowd becoming enlightened? Truth happens to individuals— a Tilopa, an Atisha, a Nanak, a Kabir, a Farid.

Truth happens to individuals.

Be an individual if you really want truth to happen to you.

Take all the risks that are needed to be an individual, and accept the challenges so that they can sharpen you, can give you brilliance and intelligence.

Truth is not a belief; it is utter intelligence. It is a flaring-up of

21

the hidden sources of your life; it is an enlightening experience of your consciousness. But you will have to provide the right space for it to happen. And the right space is accepting yourself as you are. Don't deny anything, don't become split, don't feel guilty.

Rejoice! And I say to you again, rejoice as you are.

I am always afraid of being alone, because when I am alone, I start to wonder who I am. It feels that if I inquire deeper, I will find out that I am not the person I have believed I was for the past twenty-six years, but a being, present at the moment of birth and maybe also the moment before. For some reason, this scares me completely. It feels like a kind of insanity, and makes me lose myself in outside things in order to feel safer. Who am I, and why the fear?

It is not only your fear, but everybody's fear as well. Because nobody is what he was meant by existence to be. The society, the culture, the religion, the education have all been conspiring against innocent children. They have all the powers—the child is helpless and dependent, so whatsoever they want to make out of him, they manage to do it. They don't allow any child to grow to his natural destiny. Their every effort is to make human beings into utilities.

Who knows, if a child is left on his own to grow, whether he will be of any use to the vested interests or not? The society is not prepared to take the risk. It grabs the child and starts molding him or her into something that is needed by the society. In a certain sense, it kills the soul of the child and gives him a false identity so that he never misses his soul, his being. The false identity is a substitute. But that substitute is useful only in the same crowd that has given it to you. The moment you are alone, the false starts falling apart and the repressed real starts expressing itself. Hence the fear of being alone.

Nobody wants to be lonely. Everybody wants to belong to a crowd—not only one crowd, but many crowds. A person belongs to a religious crowd, a political party, a Rotary Club . . . and there are many other small groups to belong to. One wants to be supported twenty-four hours a day because the false, without support, cannot stand. The moment one is alone, one starts feeling a strange craziness. That's what you are asking about—because for twenty-six years you believed yourself to be somebody, and then suddenly in a moment of loneliness you start feeling you are not that. It creates fear: then who are you?

And twenty-six years of suppression . . . it will take some time for the real to express itself.

The gap between the two has been called by the mystics "the dark night of the soul"—a very appropriate expression. You are no longer the false and you are not yet the real. You are in limbo; you don't know who you are.

Particularly in the West—and the questioner comes from the West—the problem is even more complicated. Because the West has not developed any methodology to discover the real as soon as possible, so that the dark night of the soul can be shortened. The West knows nothing as far as meditation is concerned. And meditation is only a name for being alone, silent, waiting for the real to assert itself. It is not an act, it is a silent relaxation—because whatever you "do" will come out of your false personality. All your doing for twenty-six years has come out of it; it is an old habit.

Habits die hard.

There was one great mystic in India, Eknath. He was going for a holy pilgrimage with all his disciples; it was to be a journey of three to six months. One man came to him, fell at his feet, and said, "I know I am not worthy. You know it, too—everybody knows me. But I know your compassion is greater than my unworthiness. Please accept me also as one of the members of the group that is going on the holy pilgrimage."

Eknath said, "You are a thief—and not an ordinary thief, but a master thief. You have never been caught, despite the fact that everybody knows you are a thief. I certainly feel like taking you with me, but I also have to think about those fifty people going with me. You will have to promise me—and I am not asking for more, just for these three to six months' time while we are on the pilgrimage—that you will not steal. After that, it is up to you. Once we are back home, you are free from the promise."

The man said, "I am absolutely ready to promise, and I am tremendously grateful for your compassion."

The other fifty people were suspicious. To trust in a thief?... But they could not say anything to Eknath; he was the master. The pilgrimage started, and from the very first night there was trouble. The next morning there was chaos: somebody's coat was missing, somebody's shirt was missing, somebody's money was gone. And everybody was shouting, "Where is my money? Where is my coat?" and they were all telling Eknath, "We were worried from the very beginning that you were taking this man with you. A lifelong habit..." But then they started looking, and they found that things were not really stolen. Somebody's money was missing, but it was found in somebody else's bag. Somebody's coat was missing, but it was found in somebody else's luggage. Everything was found, but it was an unnecessary trouble—every morning! And nobody could imagine what could be the meaning of it? Certainly it is not the thief, because nothing was actually stolen.

On the third night, Eknath remained awake to see what went on. In the middle of the night, the thief—just out of habit—woke up and started taking things from one place to another place. Eknath stopped him and said, "What are you doing? Have you forgotten your promise?"

He said, "No, I have not forgotten my promise. I am not stealing anything! But I have not promised that I will not move things from one place to another place. After six months, I will have to be a thief again; this is just practice. And you must understand that it is a lifelong habit, and I cannot drop it just like that. Just give me time. You should understand my problem also. For three days, I have not stolen a single thing—it is just like fasting! This is just a substitute; I am keeping myself busy. This is my usual business time, in the middle of the night, so it is very hard for me just to lie down in bed. I am awake, and so many idiots are sleeping . . . and I am not doing any harm to anybody. In the morning, they will find their things."

Eknath said, "You are a strange man. You see that every morning there is such chaos, and one or two hours unnecessarily are wasted in finding things, figuring out where you have put them, whose thing has gone into whose luggage. Everybody has to open everything and ask everybody, 'To whom does this belong?' "

The thief said, "This much concession you have to give to me."

Twenty-six years of a false personality—imposed by people whom you loved, whom you respected, and they were not intentionally doing anything bad to you. Their intentions were good; just their awareness was nil. They were not conscious people. Your parents, your teachers, your priests, your politicians were not conscious people; they were unconscious. And even a good intention in the hands of an unconscious person turns out to be poisonous.

So whenever you are alone, a deep fear arises because suddenly the false starts disappearing. And the real will take a little time. You have lost it twenty-six years back; you will have to give some consideration to the fact that a twenty-six-year gap has to be bridged.

In the fear that "I am losing myself, my senses, my sanity, my mind, everything"—because the self that has been given to you by others consists of all these things—it looks like you will go insane. You immediately start doing something just to keep yourself engaged. If there are no people, at least there is some action you can do so that the false remains engaged and does not start disappearing.

Hence people find it the most difficult on holidays. For five days they work, hoping that on the weekend they are going to relax. But the weekend is the worst time in the whole world—more accidents happen on the weekend, more people commit suicide, more murders, more stealing, more rape. Strange ... these people were engaged for five days and there was no problem. But the weekend suddenly gives them a choice, either to be engaged in something or to relax—but relaxing is fearsome; the false personality disappears. Keep engaged; do anything stupid. People are running toward the beaches, bumper to bumper, miles-long traffic. If you ask them where they are going, they are "getting away from the crowd." And the whole crowd is going with them! They are going to find a solitary, silent space—all of them.

In fact, if they had remained at home, it would have been more solitary and silent, because all the idiots have gone in search of a solitary place. And they are rushing like mad, because two days will be finished soon, they have to reach—just don't ask where! And on the beaches, you see . . . they are so crowded, not even market-places are so crowded. And strangely enough, people are feeling very much at ease, taking a sunbath. Ten thousand people on a small beach taking a sunbath, relaxing.

The same person on the same beach alone will not be able to re-lax. But he knows thousands of other people are relaxing all around him. The same people were in the offices, the same people were in the streets, the same people were in the marketplace, now the same people are on the beach. The crowd is essential for the false self to exist. The moment it is lonely, you start freaking out.

This is where one should understand a little bit of meditation.

Don't be worried, because that which can disappear is worth disappearing. It is meaningless to cling to it: it is not yours; it is not you. You are the one when the false has gone and the fresh, the innocent, the unpolluted being arises in its place.

Nobody else can answer your question "Who am I?"—only you will know it.

All meditative techniques are a help to destroy the false. They don't give you the real; the real cannot be given.

That which can be given cannot be real. The real you have al-ready; just the false has to be taken away.

In a different way, it can be said: the master takes away things from you that you don't really have, and he gives you that which you really do have.

Meditation is just a courage to be silent and alone. Slowly, slowly, you start feeling a new quality to yourself, a new aliveness, a new beauty, a new intelligence—which is not borrowed from anybody, which is growing within you. It has roots in your existence, and if you are not a coward, it will come to flowering, to fruition.

Only the brave, the courageous, the people who have guts, can be religious. Not the churchgoers—these are the cowards. Not the Hindus, not the Mohammedans, not the Christians—they are against searching. It is all the same crowd, and they are trying to make their false identity more consolidated.

You were born. You have come into the world with life, with consciousness, with tremendous sensitivity. Just look at a small child. Look at his eyes, the freshness. All that has been covered by a false personality.

There is no need to be afraid. You can lose only that which has to be lost. And it is good to lose it soon, because the longer it stays, the stronger it becomes. And one does not know anything about tomorrow. Don't die before realizing your authentic being.

Only those few people are fortunate who have lived with authentic being, and who have died with authentic being—because they know that life is eternal, and death is a fiction.

I have questions, but they are never complete,
and I don't know how to ask.

No question is ever complete, because the completion of a question will mean it has its answer in itself. A question by its very nature is incomplete. It is a desire, a longing, an inquiry, because something needs to be completed.

It is part of human consciousness that it demands completion. Leave anything incomplete and it becomes an obsession; complete it and you are free of it. Completion brings freedom.

Hence, it is not only your questions that are incomplete. You are more alert in that you have seen the incompleteness of each question.

Secondly, you don't know what to ask. Nobody knows! All our questions are out of our ignorance, out of our unconscious, out of our dark soul. Nobody knows exactly what his question is, what is essential to be asked—because the moment you know what your question is, you will immediately find the answer within yourself.

To be absolutely confident about the question means the answer is not very far. It is very close, because confidence comes from the answer, not from the question.

But still, a person has to ask. Although all questions are incomplete and you do not know what to ask, still everybody has to ask because people cannot remain silent. It is possible not to ask—that does not mean you don't have questions, that simply means you are not bringing them out. Perhaps you are afraid to be exposed, because each question will reveal your ignorance.

There are millions of people who never ask, for the simple reason that to be silent at least appears to be wise. To ask the question is to show your wounds, is to show all the dark spots in your being. It needs courage.

Third, there are questions that are not out of your ignorance but out of your borrowed knowledge—which are the worst questions possible.

A question that comes out of ignorance is innocent, has purity. It is unpolluted, uncorrupted; it shows your courage, your trust. But there are questions that come out of your borrowed knowledge. You have heard much, you have read much, you have been informed from the parents, teachers, priests, politicians—all kinds of demagogues, all kinds of pretenders to knowledge—and you have been collecting all their garbage.

A friend has sent me a beautiful present, a very artistic, beautiful wastepaper basket with a note—"Osho, if you feel my questions are just garbage, throw them in this wastepaper basket. You need not answer them."

Questions coming out of knowledge are garbage.

You don't know anything about God, the universe; you don't know anything about the soul, reincarnation, future lives, past lives. All that you know is simply hearsay. People have been chattering around you, and you are collecting all kinds of information that seems to be important to you. Why does it seem important?—it seems important because it covers your ignorance. It helps you to feel as if you know. But remember, it is a very big *as if*. You do not know, it is only *as if*.

All holy scriptures, all books on philosophy, all theology should be categorized into one category: *as if*. They are talking about every possible impossible thing they know nothing of! But they are articulate, imaginative intellectuals who can create systems out of nothing.

That's why no philosopher agrees with any other philosopher. And every philosopher thinks that he has found the whole system that explains everything in the world—all the other philosophers laugh at him; they find thousands of loopholes in his system. But as far as they themselves are concerned, they commit the same mistake: they claim that their system is complete and now there is no question of further inquiry.

And the strangest thing is that these are the people who are very insightful in seeing the loopholes of others, but they cannot see the loopholes of their own system. Perhaps they don't want to see. They are there, everybody else can see them; it is impossible that they themselves are not seeing them. They are ignoring them, hoping that nobody else sees them.

Every philosophy has failed. Every religion has failed. You are carrying the ruins of all the philosophies and all the religions in your mind, and out of those ruins, questions arise. Those questions are meaningless; you should not ask them. They really show your stupidity.

But questions arising out of your ignorance—just like a child asking—those questions are incomplete, not very great questions, but tremendously important.

One day, a small child was walking with D. H. Lawrence in a garden, and was continually asking questions of all kinds. And D. H. Lawrence was one of the most sincere men of his time, condemned by governments, by priests because of his sincerity, because he would say only the truth, because he was not ready to be diplomatic, a hypocrite, because he would not compromise. Even before this small child he showed such authentic sincerity, which even your great saints have not shown.

The child asked, "Why are the trees green?"—a very simple question, but very profound. All the trees are green—why? What is the matter with the trees? When there are so many colors, when the whole rainbow of colors is available—some tree can be yellow, some tree can be red, some tree can be blue—why have all the trees chosen to be green?

In D. H. Lawrence's place, any parent, any teacher, any priest, anybody—*x, y, z*—would have told some lie: "God made them green because green is very soothing to the eyes." But this would have been deceptive, a lie. And D. H. Lawrence knows that he does not know anything about God, does not know why the trees are green.

In fact, not even a scientist who has been working with the trees knows, although he can show that it is because of a certain element, chlorophyll, that trees are green. But that is not the answer for a child. He will simply ask, "Why have they chosen chlorophyll—all the trees?" It is not a satisfactory answer.

D. H. Lawrence closed his eyes, waited for a moment in silence. . . . What to say to this child? He did not want to be deceptive to an innocent child—although the question is ordinary, any answer would do. But the question has come from innocence; hence it is very profound. And D. H. Lawrence opened his eyes, looked at the trees, and said to the child, "The trees are green because they are green."

The child said, "Right. I was also thinking that."

But D. H. Lawrence remembered it in his memoirs: "To me it was a great experience—the love and the trust the child showed towards me because of sheer sincerity. My answer was not an answer; according to logicians, it was a tautology. 'The trees are green because they are green'—is this an answer?"

In fact, D. H. Lawrence is accepting it: "My child, I am as ignorant as you are. Just because there is a difference of age does not mean that I know and you do not know." The difference of age is not the difference between ignorance and knowledge.

Trees being green is part of the mystery of the whole existence. Things are what they are. A woman is a woman; a man is a man. A rose is a rose; call it by any name, it still remains a rose.

That morning, in that small incident, something tremendously beautiful is hidden.

Ask questions—not out of knowledge, because all that knowledge is borrowed, unfounded, pure rubbish.

Ask out of your ignorance.

Remember, the ignorance is yours—be proud of it.

The knowledge is not yours. How can you be proud of it?

And the question is not to cover the ignorance. The question is to bring some light, so that the ignorance, the darkness, disappears.

I cannot give you any better answer than D. H. Lawrence, but I can give you something else, which Lawrence has no insight about. I can give you a space, a silence in which you can realize the mystery on your own.

You just ask the question, whatever the question is. Just remember: Don't ask out of knowledge—ask out of your own authentic ignorance.

And my answers are not answers, in fact. My answers are killers—they simply kill the question, they take away the question, they don't give you any answer to hold on to.

And that is the difference between a teacher and a master: the teacher gives you answers so that you can hold those answers and remain ignorant—beautifully decorated on the surface, libraries full of answers, but underneath, below the surface, an abysmal ignorance. The master simply kills your questions. He does not give you an answer; he takes away the question.

If all your questions can be taken away . . . listen carefully to what I am saying:

If all your questions can be taken away, your ignorance is

bound to disappear, and what remains is innocence. And innocence is a light unto itself.

In that innocence, you don't know any question, any answer, because the whole realm of questions and answers is left behind. It has become irrelevant; you have transcended it. You are pure of questions and pure of answers. This state is enlightenment. And if you are courageous enough, you can go even beyond it.

This will give you all the beautiful experiences described by the mystics down the ages: Your heart will dance with ecstasy, your whole being will become a beautiful sunrise ... thousands of lotuses blossoming in you.

If you want, you can make your home here.

In the past, people have stopped here, because where can you find a better place? Gautam Buddha has called this place the Lotus Paradise.

But if you are a born seeker ...

I will suggest that you have a little rest, enjoy all the beauties of enlightenment, but don't make it a full stop.

Go beyond, because life, its journey, is unending and much more is going to happen that is absolutely indescribable.

The experience of enlightenment is also beyond description, but it has been described by all who have experienced it. They all say it is beyond description and still they describe it—that it is full of light, that it is full of joy, that it is the ultimate in blissfulness. If this is not description, then what is description?

I am saying it for the first time: For thousands of years, the people who have become enlightened have been saying that it cannot be described, and at the same time have been describing it, have been their whole lives singing it. But beyond enlightenment, you certainly enter into a world that is indescribable. Because in enlightenment you still are; otherwise, who is feeling the blissfulness, who is seeing the light? Kabir says, ". . . as if thousands of suns have risen." Who is seeing it?

Enlightenment is the ultimate experience—but still it is experience, and the experiencer is there.

Going beyond it, there is no experiencer.

You dissolve.

First you were trying to dissolve your problems; now *you* dissolve—because existentially you are the problem. Your separation from existence is the only question that has to be solved.

You lose your boundaries; you are no more. Who is there to experience?

You need tremendous courage to drop the ego to achieve enlightenment. You will need a million times more courage to drop yourself to attain the beyond—and the beyond is the real.

2

In Search of Meaning

L ife is in living. It is not a thing; it is a process. There is no way to attain life except by living it, except by being alive, by flowing, streaming with it. If you are seeking the meaning of life in some dogma, in some philosophy, in some theology, that is the sure way to miss life and meaning both.

Life is not somewhere waiting for you; it is happening in you. It is not in the future as a goal to be arrived at; it is here now, this very moment—in your breathing, circulating in your blood, beating in your heart.

What do I want?

Nobody knows exactly, because nobody is even aware of who he is. The question of wanting is secondary; the basic question is, Who are you? Out of that, things can be settled—what your desires, your wants, your ambitions will be.

If you are an ego, then of course you want money, power, prestige. Then your life will have a political structure. You will be in constant struggle with other people, you will be competitive—ambition means competition. You will be continuously at others' throats and they will be continuously at your throat. Then life becomes what Charles Darwin says, the survival of the fittest. In fact, his use of the word *fittest* is not right. What he really means by the fittest is the most cunning, the most animal-like, the most stubborn, the most ugly. Charles Darwin will not say that Buddha is the fittest, or that Jesus or Socrates is the fittest. These people were killed so easily, and the people who killed them survived. Jesus could not survive, so according to Darwin, Jesus is not the fittest person. Pontius Pilate is far more fit, more on the right track. Socrates is not the fittest, but the people who poisoned him, who condemned him to death, are. Darwin's use of the word *fittest* is unfortunate.

If you are living in the ego, then your life will be a struggle; it will be violent, aggressive. You will create misery for others and misery for yourself, too, because a life of conflict cannot be anything else. So it all depends on you, who you are.

If you are the ego, still thinking of yourself in terms of the ego, then you will have a certain stinking quality. Or if you have come to understand that you are not the ego, then your life will have a fragrance. If you don't know yourself, you are living out of unconsciousness, and a life of unconsciousness can only be one of misunderstanding. You may listen to Buddha, you may listen to me, you may listen to Jesus, but you will interpret according to your own unconsciousness—you will *mis*interpret.

Christianity is the misinterpretation of Jesus, so is Buddhism the misinterpretation of Buddha, and so is Jainism the misinterpretation of Mahavira. All these religions are misinterpretations, distortions, because the people who follow Buddha, Mahavira, Krishna, are ordinary people without any awareness. Whatsoever they do, they will save the letter and kill the spirit.

A philosopher was walking around a park and noticed a man sitting in the lotus posture, eyes open, looking at the ground. The philosopher saw that the man was totally absorbed in his gazing downward. After watching him for a long time, the philosopher could no longer resist and went over to the strange fellow, asking, "What are you looking for? What are you doing?"

The man answered without shifting his gaze, "I am following the Zen tradition of sitting silently doing nothing and then the spring comes and the grass grows by itself. I am trying to watch the grass growing, and it is not growing at all!"

There is no need to watch the grass growing—but that's what always happens. Jesus says one thing, people hear it, but they hear only the words and they give those words their own meaning.

A mother took her small son to the psychiatrist and for at least three hours told the psychiatrist the whole story of her son. The psychiatrist was getting tired, fed up, but the woman was so absorbed in the telling that she was not even giving the psychiatrist an opportunity to prevent her. One sentence followed another with no gap.

Finally the psychiatrist had to say, "Please, now stop! Let me ask the son something!"

And he asked the son, "Your mother is complaining that you don't listen to anything she says to you. Have you difficulty in hearing?"

The son said, "No, I have no difficulty hearing—my ears are perfectly okay—but as far as *listening* is concerned, now you can judge for yourself. Can you listen to my mother? Hear I can; I *have* to. I have been watching you—even you were fidgeting. One has to hear, but *listening*—at least I am free to listen or not. Whether I listen or not, that is up to me. If she is shouting at me, hearing it is inevitable, but listening is a totally different matter."

You have heard but you have not listened, and all kinds of distortions have gathered around. And people go on repeating those words without any idea of what they are repeating.

You ask me, "What do I want?" I should ask you, rather than you asking me, because it depends where you are. If you are identified with the body, then your wants will be different; then food and sex will be your only wants, your only desires. These two are animal desires, the lowest. I am not condemning them by calling them the lowest, I am not evaluating them, remember. I am just stating a fact: it is the lowest rung of the ladder. If you are identified with the mind, your desires will be different: music, dance, poetry, and then there are thousands of things. . . .

The body is very limited; it has simple preoccupations: food and sex. It moves like a pendulum between these two, food and sex, and there is nothing more to it. But if you are identified with the mind, then the mind has many dimensions. You can be interested in philosophy, you can be interested in science, you can be interested in religion—you can be interested in as many things as you can imagine.

If you are identified with the heart, then your desires will be of a still higher nature, higher than the mind. You will become more aesthetic, more sensitive, more alert, more loving. The mind is aggressive; the heart is receptive. The mind is male; the heart is female. The mind is logic; the heart is love.

So it depends where you are stuck: at the body, at the mind, at the heart. These are the three most important places from which one can function. But there is also a fourth in you; in the East it is called *turiya*. *Turiya* simply means "the fourth," the transcendental. If you are aware of your transcendentalness, then all desires disappear. Then one simply is, with no desire at all, with nothing to be asked, to be fulfilled. There is no future and no past. Then one lives just in the moment, utterly contented, fulfilled. In the fourth, your one-thousand-petaled lotus opens up; you become divine.

You are asking me, "What do I want?" That simply shows you don't even know where you are, where you are stuck. You will have to inquire within yourself—and it is not very difficult. If it is food and sex that take up the major part of your energy, then that is where you are identified. If it is something concerned with thinking, then it is the mind; if it is concerned with feeling, then it is the heart.

And, of course it cannot be the fourth; otherwise the question would not have arisen at all!

So rather than answering you, I would like to ask *you* where you are. Inquire!

Three pigs entered a bar. The first pig ordered a drink and then asked the way to the bathroom. The second pig ordered a drink and also asked the bartender the way to the bathroom. Then the third pig came up to the bar and ordered a drink.

"Don't you want to know where the bathroom is?" sneered the bartender.

"No!" replied the little pig. "I am the one that goes, 'Wee, wee, wee . . . all the way home!'"

I should ask you: Where are you? What kind of identification do you have? Where are you stuck? Only then can things be clear—and it is not difficult.

But it happens again and again that people ask beautiful questions, and particularly the Indians. They may be stuck at their sex center, but they will ask about *samadhi*. They will ask, "What is *nirvikalpa samadhi*, where all thoughts disappear, that thoughtless consciousness? What is it? What is *nirbeej samadhi*, the seedless, where even the seeds for any future are completely burnt? What is that ultimate state when one need not return to the earth, to the womb, to life again?" These are just foolish questions they are asking; they are not their own questions. They are not at all concerned with their real situation. They are asking beautiful questions, metaphysical, esoteric, to show that they are higher-quality beings; that they are scholarly, that they know the scriptures, that they are seekers; that they are not ordinary people—they are extraordinary, religious. That is driving the Indians into more and more of a mess.

It is always good to ask something that is relevant to you rather than to ask something that is of no concern to you. People ask me whether God exists or not, and they don't even know whether *they* exist or not!

So it is always good to ask realistic questions, because then it can be of some help to you. If you are suffering from the common cold and you go to the physician and you ask about cancer . . . because a man like you, how can he suffer from such an ordinary thing as the common cold? . . . Every ordinary person suffers from the common cold; that's why it is called the *common* cold. But you are such an uncommon person—you are not any Tom, Harry, or Dick. You are so special, you have to suffer from something very special, so you ask a question about cancer. And if the physician helps you in curing the cancer, you will get into more trouble—that treatment is not going to fit you at all. It will create more complications in you because those medicines can kill you, because there is nothing for them to work upon; there is no cancer in you and they cannot be of any use for the common cold.

In fact, for the common cold there is no medicine. If you take medicine, the common cold goes within seven days; if you don't take any, it goes within one week! In fact, it is so common that medical science has not bothered about it at all. Who cares about such small things? People are concerned about going to the moon, and about such small matters as the common cold or a leaking fountain pen, who bothers? The fountain pen still leaks! People have reached the moon and they have not yet been able to make a 100 percent guaranteed fountain pen that is not going to leak.

Just look inside yourself. Where exactly is your problem?

A general visiting a field hospital asks one of the bedridden soldiers, "What is wrong with you?"

"Sir," replies the soldier, "I've got boils."

"What treatment do you get?"

"They swab me down with iodine tincture, sir."

"And that helps?" asks the general.

"Yes, sir!" replies the soldier.

Then the general goes to the soldier in the next bed and

finds out that this guy has hemorrhoids. He, too, gets swabbed down with iodine; it helps, and he does not have any other wishes. The general then asks the third soldier, "What is wrong with you?"

"Sir, I've got swollen tonsils. I get swabbed down with iodine, and yes, it helps."

"Anything you would like?" asks the concerned general.

"Yes, sir!" replied the soldier. "I'd like to be the first to be swabbed down."

First you have to see your situation, where you are; only then can you say what you want. If you are being swabbed down with iodine tincture after these two fellows—one who has boils and one who has hemorrhoids—and you are suffering only from swollen tonsils, then the problem is clear!

Inquire, look for the exact place where you are. As far as I am concerned, all desire is a sheer waste, all wanting is wrong. But if you are identified with the body, I cannot say that to you, because that will be too far away from you. If you are identified with the body, I will say move a little toward higher desires, the desires of the mind, and then a little higher, the desires of the heart, and then ultimately to the state of desirelessness.

No desire can ever be fulfilled. This is the difference between the scientific approach and the mystic's approach. Science tries to fulfill your desires, and of course, science has succeeded in doing many things, but man remains in the same misery. The mystic tries to wake you up to that great understanding from where you can see that all desires are intrinsically unfulfillable.

One has to go beyond all desires; only then is there contentment.

Contentment is not at the end of a desire; contentment is not brought by fulfilling the desire, because the desire cannot be fulfilled. By the time you come to the fulfillment of your desire, you will find a thousand and one other desires have arisen. Each desire branches out into many new desires. And again and again it will happen, and your whole life will be wasted.

Those who have known, those who have seen—the buddhas, the awakened ones—have all agreed on one point. It is not a philosophical thing, it is factual, the fact of the inner world: that contentment is when all desires have been dropped. It is with the absence of the desires that contentment arises within you—in the absence. In fact, the very absence of desires is contentment, is fulfillment, flowering, fruition.

So move from lower desires to higher desires, from gross desires to more subtle desires, then to the subtlest, because from the subtlest, the jump into no-desire, into desirelessness, is easy. Desirelessness is nirvana.

Nirvana has two meanings. It is one of the most beautiful words; any language can be proud of this word. It has two meanings, but those two meanings are like two sides of the same coin. One meaning is cessation of the ego, and the other meaning is cessation of all desires. It happens simultaneously. The ego and the desires are intrinsically together, they are inseparably together. The moment ego dies, desires disappear, or vice versa: the moment desires are transcended, ego is transcended. And to be desireless, to be egoless, is to know the ultimate bliss, is to know the eternal ecstasy.

Is there any point in living?

Man has been brought up by all the traditions in a schizophrenic way. It was helpful for those traditions to divide man in every possible dimension, and create a conflict between the divisions. This way man becomes weak, shaky, fearful, ready to submit, surrender; ready to be enslaved by the priests, by the politicians, by anybody.

This question also arises out of a schizophrenic mind. It will be a little difficult for you to understand because you may never have thought that the division between ends and means is a basic strategy of creating a split in man.

Has living any meaning, any point, any worth? That is the question you are asking. Is there some goal to be achieved by life, by living? Is there some place you will reach one day by living? Living is a means. The goal, the attainment, somewhere far away, is the end. And that end will make it meaningful. If there is no end, then certainly life is meaningless; a God is needed to make your life meaningful. First create the division between ends and means. That divides your mind.

Your mind is always asking, Why? For what? And anything that has no answer to the question, "For what?" slowly becomes of no value to you. That's how love has become valueless. What point is there in love? Where is it going to lead you? What is going to be the achievement out of it? Will you attain to some utopia, some paradise?

Of course, love has no point in that way. It is pointless.

What is the point of beauty? You see a sunset—you are stunned, it is so beautiful, but any idiot can ask the question, "What is the meaning of it?" and you will be without any answer.

And if there is no meaning, then why, unnecessarily, are you bragging about beauty?

A beautiful flower, or a beautiful painting, or beautiful music, beautiful poetry—they don't have any point. They are not arguments to prove something; neither are they means to achieve any end.

And living consists only of those things that are pointless.

Let me repeat it: Living consists only of those things that have no point at all, which have no meaning at all—in the sense that they don't have any goal, that they don't lead you anywhere, that you don't get anything out of them.

In other words, living is significant in itself. The means and ends are together, not separate.

But that is the strategy of all those who have been lustful for power, down the ages. They say that means are means, and ends are ends. Means are useful because they lead you to the end. If they don't lead to an end, they are meaningless. In this way, they have destroyed all that is really significant, and they have imposed things on you that are absolutely insignificant.

Money has a point. A political career has a point. To be religious has a point, because that is the means to heaven, to God. Business has a point because immediately you see the end result. Business became important, politics became important, religion became important, and poetry, music, dancing, love, friendliness, beauty, truth, all disappeared from your life. It is a simple strategy, but it destroyed all that makes you significant, that gives ecstasy to your being. But the schizophrenic mind will ask, "What is the point of ecstasy?"

People have asked me, hundreds of people, "What is the meaning of meditation? What will we gain out of it? First, it is very difficult to attain—and even if we attain it, what is going to be the end result?"

It is very difficult to explain to these people that meditation is an end in itself. There is no end beyond it.

Anything that has an end beyond it is just for the mediocre mind. And anything that has its end in itself is for the really intelligent person. You will see the mediocre person becoming the president of a country, the prime minister of a country; becoming the richest man in the country, becoming the pope, becoming the head of a religion. But these are all mediocre people; their only qualification is their mediocrity. They are third rate, and basically they are schizophrenic. They have divided their life in two parts: ends and means.

My approach is totally different:

To make you one single whole.

So I want you to live just for life's sake.

The poets have defined art as for its own sake, there is nothing else beyond it: "art for art's sake." It will not appeal to the mediocre at all, because he counts things in terms of money, position, power. Is your poetry going to make you the prime minister of the country? Then it is meaningful. But in fact, your poetry may make you just a beggar, because who is going to purchase your poetry?

I am acquainted with many kinds of geniuses who are living like beggars for the simple reason that they did not accept the mediocre way of life, and they did not allow themselves to become schizophrenic. They are *living* – and of course they have a joy that no politician can ever know: they have a certain radiance that no billionaire is going to know. They have a certain rhythm to their heart of which these so-called religious people have no idea. But as far as the outside is concerned, they have been made by the society to live like beggars.

I would like you to remember perhaps the greatest painter, Vincent van Gogh. His father wanted him to become a religious minister, to live a life of respect, comfortable, convenient—and not only in this world, in the other world after death, too. But Vincent van Gogh wanted to become a painter. His father said, "You are mad!"

He said, "That may be. To me, you are mad. I don't see any significance in becoming a minister, because everything I would say would be nothing but lies. I don't know God. I don't know whether there is any heaven or hell. I don't know whether man survives after death or not. I will be continually telling lies. Of course it is respectable, but that kind of respect is not for me. I would not be rejoicing in it; it would be a torture to my soul." The father threw him out.

He started painting—he is the first modern painter. You can draw a line at Vincent van Gogh: before him, painting was ordinary. Even the greatest painters, like Michelangelo, are of minor importance compared to Vincent van Gogh, because what they were painting was ordinary. Their painting was for the marketplace. Michelangelo was painting for churches his whole life; painting on church walls and church ceilings. He broke his backbone painting church ceilings, because to paint a ceiling, you have to lie down on a high platform while you paint. It is a very uncomfortable position, and for days together, months together . . . But he was earning money, and he was earning respect. He was painting angels,

Christ, God creating the world. His most famous painting is of God creating the world.

Vincent van Gogh opens a totally new dimension. He could not sell a single painting in his whole life. Now, who will say that his painting has any point? Not a single person could see that there was anything in his paintings. His younger brother used to send him money; enough so that he did not die of starvation, just enough for food every week—because if he gave him enough for a whole month, he would finish it within two or three days, and the remaining days he would be starving. So every week, he would send money to him.

And what Vincent van Gogh did, was that for four days he would eat, and for three days in between those four days, he would save the money for paints, canvases. This is something totally different from Michelangelo, who earned enough money, who became a rich person. He sold all his paintings. They were made to be sold; it was business. Of course, he was a great painter, so even paintings that were created to be sold came out beautifully. But if he had had the guts of a Vincent van Gogh, he would have enriched the whole world.

Three days starving, and Van Gogh would use the money to purchase paints and canvases. His younger brother, hearing that not a single painting had sold, gave some money to a man—a friend of his not known to Vincent van Gogh—and told him to go and purchase at least one painting: "That will give him some satisfaction. The poor man is dying; the whole day he is painting, starving for his painting, but nobody is ready to purchase even one—nobody sees anything in what he does." Because to see something in Vincent van

Gogh's painting, you need the eye of a painter of the caliber of Van Gogh; less than that will not do.

His paintings seemed strange to people. His trees are painted so high that they go above the stars; stars are left far behind. Now, you will think that this man is mad . . . trees going up higher than the stars? Have you seen such trees anywhere? When Vincent van Gogh was asked, "Your trees always go beyond the stars?" he said, "Yes, because I understand trees. I have felt always that trees are the ambition of the earth to reach the stars. Otherwise, why? To touch the stars, to feel the stars, to go beyond the stars—this is the desire of the earth. The earth tries hard, but cannot fulfill the desire. I can do it. The earth will understand my paintings, and I don't care about you, whether you understand or not."

Now, this kind of painting you cannot sell. The man sent by his brother came, and Van Gogh was very happy: at last somebody had come to purchase a painting! But soon his happiness turned to despair because the man just walked in, picked one painting, and gave him the money.

Vincent van Gogh said, "But do you understand the painting? You have picked it up so casually, you have not looked; I have hundreds of paintings. You have not even bothered to look around; you have simply picked one that was accidentally in front of you. I suspect that you are sent by my brother. Put the painting back, and take your money. I will not sell the painting to a man who has no eyes for it. And tell my brother never to do such a thing again."

The man was puzzled how he managed to figure it out. He said, "You don't know me, how did you figure it out?"

He said, "That's too simple. I know my brother wants me to have some consolation. He must have arranged for you to come—

and this money belongs to him—because I can see that you are blind as far as paintings are concerned. And I am not one to sell paintings to blind people; I cannot exploit a blind man and sell him a painting. What will he do with it? And tell my brother also that he also does not understand painting, otherwise he would not have sent you."

When the brother came to know, he came to apologize. He said, "Instead of giving you a little consolation, I have wounded you. I will never do such a thing again."

His whole life, Van Gogh was just giving his paintings to friends. To the hotel where he used to eat four days a week, he would present a painting, or to a prostitute who had once said to him that he was a beautiful man. To be absolutely factual, he was ugly. No woman ever fell in love with him; it was impossible. This prostitute out of compassion—and sometimes prostitutes have more compassion than your so-called ladies, they understand men more—just out of compassion, she said, "I like you very much." He had never heard this. Love was a faraway thing. Even liking . . .

He said, "Really, you like me? What do you like in me?" Now, the woman was at a loss.

She said, "I like your ears. Your ears are beautiful." And you will be surprised that Van Gogh went home, cut off one of his ears with a razor, packed it beautifully, went to the prostitute, and gave his ear to her. And blood was flowing. . . .

She said, "What have you done?"

He said, "Nobody ever liked anything in me. And I am a poor man, how can I thank you? You liked my ears; I have presented one of them to you. If you had liked my eyes, I would have presented one to you. If you had liked me, I would have died for you."

The prostitute could not believe it. But for the first time, Van Gogh was happy, smiling; somebody had liked at least a part of him. And that woman had just said it jokingly—otherwise who bothers about your ears? If people like something, they like your eyes, they like your nose, your lips—you won't hear lovers talking about each other's ears.

Only in ancient Hindu scriptures on sexology, the *Kamasutras* of Vatsyayana . . . That is the only book I have found that can be connected to this incident with Vincent van Gogh, because only Vatsyayana says, "Very few people are aware that earlobes are tremendously sexual and sensitive points in the body. Lovers should play with each other's earlobes."

So this prostitute perhaps was aware . . . because prostitutes become aware of many things that ordinary women and men don't become aware of, because they come in contact with so many people. Perhaps she was aware that ears have a sexual significance. They certainly have. Vatsyayana is one of the greatest experts. Freud and Havelock Ellis and other sexologists are just pygmies before Vatsyayana. And when he says something, he means it.

Van Gogh lived his whole life in poverty. He died painting. Before dying he went mad, because for one year continually he was painting the sun: hundreds of paintings, but nothing was coming to the point he wanted. But the whole day standing in the hottest place in France, in Arles, with the sun on the head—because without the experience, how can you paint? He painted the final painting, but he went mad. Just the heat, the hunger . . . but he was immensely happy; even in madness he was painting. And those paintings he did in the madhouse are now worth millions.

He committed suicide for the simple reason—that he had

painted everything that he wanted to paint. Now painting was finished; he had come to a dead end. There was nothing more to do. Now to go on living was occupying space, somebody's place; that was ugly to him.

That's what he wrote in his letters to his brother: "My work is done. I have lived tremendously—the way I wanted to live. I have painted what I wanted to paint. My last painting I have done today, and now I am taking a jump from this life into the unknown, whatever it is, because this life no longer contains anything for me."

Will you consider this man a genius? Will you consider this man intelligent, wise? No, ordinarily you would think he is simply mad. But I cannot say that. His living and his painting were not two things: painting was his living; that was his life. So to the whole world it seems suicide—not to me. To me it simply seems a natural end. The painting is completed. Life is fulfilled. There was no other goal; whether he receives the Nobel Prize or whether anybody appreciates his painting means nothing.

In his lifetime, nobody appreciated his work. In his lifetime, no art gallery accepted his paintings, even for free. After he died, slowly, because of his sacrifice, painting changed its whole flavor. There would have been no Picasso without Vincent van Gogh. All the painters that have come after Vincent van Gogh are indebted to him, incalculably, because that man changed the whole direction.

Slowly, slowly, as the direction changed, his paintings were discovered. A great search was made. People had thrown his paintings in their empty houses, or in their basements, thinking they were useless. They rushed to their basements, discovered his paintings, cleaned them. Even faked paintings came onto the market as authentic Van Gogh works. Now there are only two hundred paintings; he must have painted thousands. But any art gallery that has a Vincent van Gogh is proud, because the man poured his whole life into his paintings. They were not painted with color but with blood, breath—his heartbeat is there.

Don't ask such a man, "Is there any meaning in your painting?" He is there in his painting, and you are asking, "Is there any meaning in your painting?" If you cannot see the meaning, it is your responsibility.

The higher a thing rises, the fewer the people who will recognize it. When something reaches the highest point, it is very difficult to find even a few people to recognize it. At the ultimate omega point, only the person himself recognizes what has happened to him; he cannot find even a second person who can see it. That's why a Buddha has to declare himself that he is enlightened. Nobody else can recognize it, because to recognize it, you will have to have some taste of it. Otherwise, how can you recognize it? No recognition is possible, because the point is so high.

But what is the meaning of buddhahood? What is the meaning of becoming enlightened? What is the point? If you ask about the point, there is none. It itself is enough. It needs nothing else to make it significant.

That's what I mean when I say that the really valuable things in life are not divided into ends and means. There is no division between ends and means. Ends are the means, means are the ends—perhaps two sides of the same coin inseparably joined together—in fact, they are a oneness, a wholeness.

You ask me, "Is there any point in life, in living?" I am afraid that if I say there is no point in living, you will think that means you have to commit suicide, because if there is no point in living, then what else to do?—commit suicide! I am not saying commit suicide, because in committing suicide also there is no point.

Living: live, and live totally. Dying: die, and die totally. And in that totality you will find significance.

I am deliberately not using the word *meaning*, and using the word *significance* because *meaning* is contaminated. The word *meaning*—it always points somewhere else. You must have heard, you must have read in your childhood, many stories. . . . Why are they written for children?—perhaps the writers don't know, but it is part of the same exploitation of humanity.

One story goes like this: There is a man whose life is in a parrot. If you kill the parrot, the man will be killed, but you cannot kill the man directly. You can shoot him and nothing will happen. You can swing your sword and the sword will pass through his neck, but the head will remain joined to the body. You cannot kill the man—first you have to find where his life is. So in those types of stories, the person's life is always somewhere else. And when you find out where it is, you just kill the parrot, and wherever the man is, he will die immediately.

Even when I was a child, I used to ask my teacher, "This seems to be a very stupid kind of story because I don't see anyone whose life is in a parrot or in a dog or in something else, like a tree." It was the first time I heard that story, that type of story; then I came across many. They were written specially for children.

The man who was teaching me was a very nice and respectable gentleman. I asked him, "Can you tell me where your life is? Because I would like to try . . ."

He said, "What do you mean?"

I said, "I would like to kill that bird in which your life is. You are an intelligent man, wise, respected. You must have put your life somewhere else so nobody can kill you."

That's what the story says—that wise people keep their life somewhere else, so that you cannot kill them, so that nobody can kill them. And it is impossible to find where they have kept their life unless they tell the secret, nobody can figure it out. This world is so big, and there are so many people and so many animals, and so many birds, and trees . . . nobody knows where that man has put his life.

"You are a wise man, respected, you must have kept your life hidden somewhere; you can just tell me in private. I will not kill the bird completely; just give him a few twists and turns, and see what happens to you."

He said, "You are a strange boy. I have been teaching this story my whole life, and you want to give me a twist and turn? This is only a story!"

But I said, "What is the point of the story? Why do you go on teaching this story and this kind of thing to children?"

He could not answer. I asked my father, "What can be the meaning of this story? Why should these things be taught, which are absolutely absurd?"

He said, "If your teacher cannot answer, then how can I answer? I don't know. He is far more educated and intelligent and wise. You harass him, rather than harassing me."

But now I know the meaning of the stories and why they are being taught to the children. These stories enter the unconscious, and the child starts thinking life is always somewhere else—in heaven, in God, always somewhere else—it is not in you. You are empty, just an empty shell. You don't have meaning in your life here now. Here you are only a means, a ladder. If you go up the ladder, perhaps someday you will find your life, your God, your goal, your meaning, whatever name you give to it.

But I say to you that you are the meaning, the significance, and living itself is intrinsically complete. Life needs nothing else to be added to it.

All that life needs is that you live it to its totality.

If you live only partially, then you will not feel the thrill of being alive.

It is like any mechanism when just a part is functioning. . . . For example, in a clock: if only the second hand is working but neither the hour hand nor the minute hand moves, what purpose will it serve? There will be movement, a certain part is working, but unless the whole works and works in harmony, there cannot be a song out of it.

And this is the situation: Everybody is living partially, a small part. So you make noise, but you can't create a song. You move your hands and legs, but no dance happens. The dance, the song, the significance comes into existence the moment you function as a whole in harmony, in accord. Then you don't ask such questions as, "Is there any point in living?" You know.

Living itself is the point. There is no other point.

But you have not been allowed to remain one and whole. You have been divided, cut into several parts. A few parts have been completely closed—so much so that you don't know even that they belong to you. Much of you has been thrown in the basement.

Much of you has been so condemned that although you know it is there, you cannot dare to accept that it is part of you—you go on denying it; you go on repressing it.

You know only a very small fragment in you, which they call "conscience," which is a social product not a natural thing, which society creates inside you to control you from inside. The constable is outside; the court is outside controlling you. And the conscience is inside, which is far more powerful.

That's why even in a court, first they will give you the Bible. You take the oath on the Bible because the court also knows that if you are a Christian, putting your hand on the Bible and saying, "I swear to tell the truth, the whole truth, and nothing but the truth," your conscience will force you to speak the truth—because now you have taken the oath in the name of God, and you have touched the Bible. If you speak a lie, you will be thrown into hell.

Before, at the most, if you were caught, you would be thrown into prison for a few months, a few years. But now you will be thrown in hell for eternity. Even the court accepts that the Bible is more powerful, the Gita is more powerful, the Koran is more powerful than the court, than the military, than the army.

Conscience is one of the meanest inventions of humanity.

And from the very first day the child is born, we start creating a conscience in him; a small part that goes on condemning anything the society does not want in you, and goes on appreciating anything that the society wants in you. You are no longer whole. The conscience continually goes on forcing you, so that you have to always look out—God is watching. Every act, every thought, God is watching, so beware!

Even in thoughts you are not allowed freedom: God is watching. What kind of Peeping Tom is this God? In every bathroom he is looking through the keyhole; he won't leave you alone even in your bathroom!

They go on talking about freedom of thought—that's all nonsense because from the very beginning, they put the foundation in every child for unfreedom of thought.

They want to control your thoughts; they want to control your dreams. They want to control everything in you. It's through a very clever device—conscience. It pricks you. It goes on telling you, "This is not right, don't do it; you will suffer." It goes on forcing you: "Do this, this is the right thing to do; you will be rewarded for it." This conscience will never allow you to be whole. It won't allow you to live as if there is nothing prohibited, as if there are no boundaries, as if you are left totally independent to be whatsoever you can be.

Then life has meaning, then living has meaning—not the meaning that is derived from ends, but the meaning that is derived from living itself. Then whatever you do, in that very doing is your reward.

For example, I am speaking to you. I am enjoying it. For thirty-five years, I have been continually speaking for no purpose. With this much speaking, I could have become a president, a prime minister; there would have been no problem in it. With so much speaking, I could have done anything. What have I gained?

But I was not out for gain in the first place—I enjoyed. This was my painting, this was my song, this was my poetry. Just those moments when I am speaking and I feel the communion happening, those moments when I see your eyes flare up, when I see that you have understood the point . . . they give me such tremendous joy that I cannot think anything can be added to it.

Action, any action done totally, with every fiber of your being in it . . . For example, if you bind my hands, I cannot speak, although there is no relationship between hands and speaking. I have tried. One day, I told a friend who was staying with me, "Tie both my hands."

He said, "What?"

I said, "Just tie them, and then ask a question."

He said, "I am always afraid to stay with you, you are crazy. And now if somebody sees that I have tied your hands and now I am asking you a question and you are answering it, what will they think?"

I said, "You forget all that. Close the door and do what I say."

So he tied both my hands to two posts, and he asked me a question. I tried in every possible way, but my hands were tied; I could not say anything to him. I simply said, "Please untie my hands."

He said, "But I cannot understand what this is all about."

I said, "It is simply that I was trying to see whether I could speak without my hands. I cannot."

What to say about hands . . . if I cross my leg on the other side—which is the way I sit in my room when I am not speaking—then something goes wrong. Then I cannot speak, because I am not at home. So the way I am sitting, the way my hands move, is a total involvement. It is not only part of me speaking, but everything in me is involved in it.

And only then can you find the intrinsic value of any act. Otherwise you have to live a life of tension, stretched between here and there, this and that faraway goal.

The pseudo-religions say, "Of course, this life is only a means, so you cannot be involved in it totally; it is only a ladder you have to use. It is not something valuable, just a stepping-stone. The real thing is there, far away." So it always remains far away. Wherever you are, the real thing will be always far away. So wherever you are, you will be missing life.

I don't have a goal.

When I was in the university, I used to go for a walk in the morning, evening, anytime.... Morning and evening absolutely, but if there was another time available, I would also go for a walk then, because the place and the trees and the road were so beautiful, and so covered with big trees from both sides that even in the hottest summer there was shadow on the road.

One of my professors who loved me very much used to watch me: that some days I would go on this road, some days on that road. There was a crossroads in the shape of a pentagon at the front gate of the university, five roads going in five directions, and he lived just near there; his were the last quarters near the gate. He asked me, "Sometimes you go on this road, sometimes on that road. Where do you go?"

I said, "I don't go anywhere. I just go for walking." If you are going somewhere, then certainly you will go on the same road; but I was not going anywhere, so it was just whimsical. I just came to the crossroads and I just used to stand there for a little while. That was making him more puzzled: how I figure it out, what I figure out standing there.

I used to figure out where the wind was blowing. Whichever way the wind was blowing, I would also go; that was my way.

"So sometimes," he would say, "you will take the same road for a week; sometimes you go only one day on some road and the next day you change. What do you do there at the crossroads? And how do you decide?"

I told him, "It is very simple. I stand there and I feel which road is alive—where the wind is blowing. I go with the wind. And it is beautiful going with the wind. I jog, I run, whatever I want to do. And the wind is there, cool, available. So I just figure it out."

Life is not going somewhere. It is just going for a morning walk.

Choose wherever your whole being is flowing, where the wind is blowing. Move on that path as far as it leads, and never expect to find anything.

Hence I have never been surprised—because I have never been expecting anything, so there is no question of surprise. Everything is surprise! And there is no question of disappointment; everything is appointment. If it happens, good; if it does not happen, even better.

Once you understand that moment-to-moment living is what real religion is all about, then you will understand why I say to drop this idea of God, heaven and hell, and all that crap. Just drop it completely because this load of so many concepts is preventing you from living moment to moment.

Live life in an organic unity. No act should be partial; you should be involved fully in it.

A Zen story:

A very curious king, wanting to know about what these people go on doing in the monasteries, asked around: "Who is the most famous master?" Finding out that the most famous master of those days was Nan-in, he went to his monastery. When he entered the monastery, he found a woodcutter. He asked him, "The monastery is so big, where can I find Master Nan-in?"

The man thought with closed eyes for a few moments, and he said, "Right now you cannot find him."

The king said, "Why can't I find him right now? Do you understand that I am the ruler of the land?"

He said, "That is irrelevant. Whoever you are, that is your business, but I assure you, you cannot find him right now."

"Is he out?" asked the king.

"No, he is in," replied the woodcutter.

The king said, "But is he involved in some work, in some ceremony, or in isolation? What is the matter?"

The man said, "He is right now cutting wood in front of you. And when I am cutting wood, I am just a woodcutter. Right now, where is Master Nan-in? I am just a woodcutter. You will have to wait."

The king thought, "This man is mad, simply mad. Master Nan-in cutting wood?" He went ahead and left the woodcutter behind, and Nan-in continued to cut wood. The winter was coming close and wood had to be stored. The king could wait, but winter wouldn't wait.

The king waited one hour, two hours—and then from the back door came Master Nan-in, in his master's robe. The king looked at him. He looked like the woodcutter!...But the king bowed down. The master sat there, and he asked, "Why have you taken so much trouble to come here?"

The king said, "There are many things, but those questions I will ask later on. First I want to know, are you the same man who was cutting wood?"

He said, "Now I am Master Nan-in. I am not the same man; the total configuration has changed. Now here I am sitting as Master Nan-in. You ask as a disciple, with humbleness, receptivity. Yes, a man very similar to me was cutting wood there, but that was a woodcutter. His name is also Nan-in."

The king was so puzzled that he left without asking the questions he had come to ask. When he went back to his court, his advisers asked what happened. He said, "What happened it is better to forget about. This Master Nan-in seems to be absolutely insane! He was cutting wood; he said, 'I am a woodcutter and Master Nan-in is not available right now.' Then the same man came in a master's robe and I asked him, and he said, 'A similar man was cutting the wood, but he was the woodcutter; I am the master.'"

One of the men in the court said, "You have missed the point of what he was trying to say to you—that when cutting wood he is totally involved in it. Nothing is left that can claim to be Master Nan-in; nothing is left out, he is just a woodcutter."

And in Zen language, which is difficult to translate, he was saying not exactly that "I am a woodcutter," he was saying, "Right now it is woodcutting"—not a woodcutter, because there is not even space for the cutter. It is simply wood being chopped, and he is so totally in it, it is only woodcutting: "Woodcutting is happening." And when he comes as a master, of course, it is a different configuration. The same parts are now in a different accord. So with each action you are a different person, if you get totally involved in it.

Buddha used to say, "It is just as the flame of the candle looks the same, but is never the same even for two consecutive moments. The flame is continuously becoming smoke, new flame is coming up. The old flame is going out; the new flame is coming up. The candle that you had burned in the evening is not the same candle that you will blow out in the morning. This is not the same flame that you had started; that has gone far away, nobody knows where. It is just a similarity of the flame that gives you the illusion that it is the same flame."

The same is true about your being.

It is a flame. It is a fire. Each moment your being is changing, and if you get involved totally in anything, then you will see the change happening in you—each moment a new being, and a new world, and a new experience. Everything suddenly becomes so full of newness that you never see the same thing twice. Then naturally, life becomes a continuous mystery, a continuous surprise. On each step a new world opens up, of tremendous meaning, of incredible ecstasy.

When death comes, death, too, is not seen as something separate from life. It is part of life, not an end of life. It is just like other happenings: love had happened, birth had happened. You were a child, and then childhood disappeared; you became a young man, and then the young man disappeared; you became an old man, and then the old man disappeared—how many things have been happening! Why don't you allow death also to happen just like other incidents?

And actually the person who has lived moment to moment lives death, too, and finds that all the moments of life can be put on one side and the one moment of death can be put on the other side, and still it weighs more. In every way it weighs more because it is the whole life condensed; and something more added to it, which was never available to you. A new door opening, with the whole life condensed: a new dimension opening.

Why does everyone want to pretend to be what they are not?
What is the psychology behind it?

Everybody is condemned from his very childhood. Whatever you do on your own accord, out of your own liking, is not acceptable. The people, the crowd in which a child has to grow has its own ideas, ideals. The child has to fit with those ideas and ideals. The child is helpless. Have you ever thought about it? The human child is the most helpless child in the whole animal kingdom. Nearly all the animals can survive without the support of the parents and the crowd, but the human child cannot survive; he will die immediately. He is the most helpless creature in the world, so vulnerable to death, so delicate. Naturally, those who are in power are able to mold the child in the way they want. So everybody has become what he is, against himself. That is the psychology behind the fact that everybody wants to pretend to be what he is not.

Everybody is in a schizophrenic state. Nobody has ever been allowed to be himself; he has been forced to be somebody else that his nature does not allow him to be happy with.

So as one grows and stands on his own legs, one starts pretending many things that one would have liked in reality to be part of one's being. But in this insane world, you have been distracted. You have been made into somebody else; you are not that. You know it. Everybody knows it—he has been forced to become a doctor, to become an engineer; he has been forced to become a politician, to become a criminal, to become a beggar.

There are all kinds of forces around.

In Mumbai, there are people whose whole business is to steal children and make them crippled, blind, lame, and force them to beg, and each evening to bring all the money they have gathered. Yes, food will be given to them, shelter will be given to them. They are being used like commodities; they are not human beings. This is the extreme, but the same has happened with everybody to a lesser or greater extent.

Nobody is at ease with himself.

I have heard about a great surgeon who was retiring, and he was very famous. He had many students and many colleagues; they all gathered, and they were dancing and singing and drinking— but he was standing in a dark corner, sad. One friend came up to him and asked, "What is the matter with you? We are celebrating and you are standing here so sad—don't you want to retire? You are seventy-five; you should have retired fifteen years ago. But because you are such a great surgeon, even at seventy-five, nobody can compete with you, nobody comes even close to you. Now, retire and relax!"

He said, "That's what I was thinking. I am feeling sad because my parents forced me to become a surgeon. I wanted to be a singer, and I would have loved it. Even if I was just a street singer, at least I would have been myself. Now I am a world-famous surgeon, but I am not myself. When people praise me as a surgeon, I listen as if they are praising somebody else. I have been given awards, honorary doctorates, but nothing rings a bell of joy in my heart, because this is not me. This being a surgeon has killed me, destroyed me.

I wanted to be just a singer, even if I had to be a beggar on the streets. But I would have been happy."

In this world, there is only one happiness, and that is to be yourself. And because nobody is himself, everybody is trying somehow to hide behind masks, pretensions, hypocrisies. They are ashamed of what they are.

We have made the world a marketplace, not a beautiful garden where everybody is allowed to bring their own flowers. We are forcing marigolds to bring roses—now from where can marigolds bring roses? Those roses will be plastic roses, and in their heart of hearts, the marigolds will be crying, and with tears, feeling ashamed that "We have not been courageous enough to rebel against the crowd. They have forced plastic flowers on us, and we have our own real flowers, for which our juices are flowing—but we cannot show our real flowers."

You are being taught everything else, but you are not taught to be yourself. This is the ugliest form of society possible, because it makes everybody miserable.

I have heard of another great man, a great professor of literature who was retiring from the university. All the university professors had gathered, all his friends had gathered, and they were rejoicing. But suddenly they became aware that he was missing. One of his friends, an attorney, went out. . . . Perhaps he in was the garden? But what was he doing there? He was sitting under a tree. The attorney was his closest friend, a boyhood friend. The attorney asked him, "What are you doing here?"

He said, "What I am doing here? Remember fifty years ago? I came to tell you that I wanted to kill my wife. And you said, 'Don't do any such thing. Otherwise you will spend fifty years in jail.' I am thinking that if I had not listened to you, today I would have been out of jail, free!" He said, "I am feeling so angry that a desire comes to me—why should I not at least kill you! Now I am seventy-five; even if they put me in jail for fifty years, they cannot keep me there that long. Within five, seven years I will be dead. But you were not a friend; you proved to be my greatest enemy."

To be what you don't want to be, to be with someone you don't want to be with, to do something you don't want to do is the basis of all your miseries. And on the one hand, the society has managed to make everybody miserable, and on the other hand, the same society expects that you should not show your misery—at least not in public, not in the open. It is your private business. And they have created it! It really is public business, not private business. The same crowd that has created all the reasons for your misery finally says to you: "Your misery is your own, so when you come out, come out smiling. Don't show your miserable face to others." This they call etiquette, manners, culture. Basically, it is hypocrisy.

And unless a person decides, "Whatever the cost, I want just to be myself. Condemned, unaccepted, losing respectability—everything is okay, but I cannot pretend anymore to be somebody else...." This decision and this declaration—this declaration of freedom, freedom from the weight of the crowd—gives birth to your natural being, to your individuality. Then you don't need any mask. Then you can be simply yourself, just as you are.

And the moment you can be just as you are, there is tremendous "peace that passeth understanding."

Research over the past few years has suggested that certain states of consciousness brought about by meditation techniques appear to evoke specific brain wave patterns. These states are now being created by electronic and auditory stimulation of the brain, and they can be learned through biofeedback.

The traditional "meditative state"—sitting silently (or at least quietly alert)—is composed of bilateral, synchronous alpha waves. Deeper meditation also has bilateral theta waves. A state called "lucid awareness" has the bilateral synchronous alpha and theta waves of deep meditation, plus the beta waves of normal thought processes. Lucid awareness can be learned through biofeedback, using the most modern equipment.

Are these kinds of stimulation and biofeedback useful tools for the meditator? What is the relationship of these technological techniques to the state of meditation that is beyond technique? Is this an example of bringing science together with meditation?

It is a very complex question. You will have to understand one of the most fundamental things about meditation—that no technique leads to meditation. The old so-called techniques and the new scientific biofeedback techniques are the same as far as meditation is concerned.

Meditation is not a by-product of any technique. Meditation happens beyond mind. No technique can go beyond mind. But there is going to be a great misunderstanding in scientific circles, and it has a certain basis. The basis of all misunderstanding is that when the being of a person is in a state of meditation, it creates certain waves in the brain. These waves can be created from the outside by technical means, but those waves will not create meditation—this is the misunderstanding.

Meditation creates those waves; it is the mind reflecting the inner world. You cannot see what is happening inside, but you can see what is happening in the brain. Now there are sensitive instruments.... We can judge what kind of waves are there when a person is asleep, what kinds of waves are there when a person is dreaming, what kinds of waves are there when a person is in meditation. But by creating the waves, you cannot create the situation—because those waves are only symptoms, indicators. It is perfectly good—you can study them. But remember that there is no shortcut to meditation, and no mechanical device can be of any help.

In fact, meditation needs no technique—scientific or otherwise. Meditation is simply an understanding. It is not a question of sitting silently; it is not a question of chanting a mantra. It is a question of understanding the subtle workings of the mind. As you understand those workings of the mind, a great awareness arises in you that is not *of* the mind. That awareness arises in your being, in your soul, in your consciousness. The mind is only a mechanism, but when that awareness arises, it is bound to create a certain energy pattern. That energy pattern is noted by the mind.

The mind is a very subtle mechanism, and you are studying from the outside—so at the most, you can study the brain. Seeing that whenever a person is silent, serene, peaceful, a certain wave pattern always, inevitably appears in the brain, the scientific thinking will say that if we can create this wave pattern in the brain, through some biofeedback technology, then the being inside will reach the heights of awareness. This is not going to happen. It is not a question of cause and effect.

These waves in the brain are not the cause of meditation; they are, on the contrary, the effect. But from the effect, you cannot move toward the cause. It is possible that with biofeedback you can create certain patterns in the brain and they will give a feeling of peace, silence, and serenity to the person. Because the person himself does not know what meditation is, and has no way of comparing, he may be misled into believing that this is meditation—but it is not. Because the moment the biofeedback mechanism stops, the waves disappear and the silence and the peace and the serenity also disappear.

You may go on practicing with those scientific instruments for years; it will not change your character, it will not change your morality, it will not change your individuality. You will remain the same.

Meditation transforms. It takes you to higher levels of consciousness and changes your whole lifestyle. It changes your reactions into responses to such an extent that it is unbelievable that the person who would have reacted in the same situation in anger is now acting in deep compassion, with love—in the same situation.

Meditation is a state of being, arrived at through understanding. It needs intelligence; it does not need techniques.

There is no technique that can give you intelligence. Otherwise, we would have changed all the idiots into geniuses; all the mediocre people would have become Albert Einsteins, Bertrand Russells, Jean-Paul Sartres. There is no way to change your intelligence from the outside, to sharpen it, to make it more penetrating, to give it more insight. It is simply a question of understanding, and nobody else can do it for you—no machine, no person.

For centuries, the so-called gurus have been cheating humanity. Now, in the future, instead of gurus, these guru machines will cheat humanity.

The gurus were cheating people by saying, "We will give you a mantra. You repeat the mantra." Certainly by repeating a mantra continuously, you create the energy field of a certain wave length; but the person chanting remains the same, because it is only on the surface. Just as you throw a pebble into the silent lake and ripples arise and move all over the lake from one corner to the other corner—but it does not touch the depths of the lake at all. The depths are completely unaware of what is happening on the surface. And what you see on the surface is also illusory. You think that ripples are moving—that's not true; nothing is moving. When you throw a pebble into the lake, it is not that ripples start moving. You can check it by putting a small flower on the water. You will be surprised to note that the flower remains in the same place. If the waves were moving and going toward the shore, they would have taken the flower with them. The flower remains where you put it. The waves are not moving; it is just the water going up and down in the same place, creating the illusion of movement. The depths of the lake will not know anything about it. And there is going to be no change in the character, in the beauty of the lake, when you create those waves.

Mind is between the world and you. Whatever happens in the world, the mind is affected by it; and you can understand through the mind what is happening outside. For example, you are seeing me—you cannot see *me*; it is your brain that is affected by certain rays and creates a picture that you interpret in the mind. You are inside, and from inside you see the picture. You don't see me; you can't see me. The brain is the mediator. As the brain is affected by the outside, the inner consciousness can read what is happening outside. And what the scientists are trying to do is just the same:

They are studying meditators and reading their wavelengths, the energy fields created by meditation. Naturally, the scientific approach is to assume that if these patterns appear, without any exception, when a person is in meditation, then we have the key; if we can create these patterns in the brain, then meditation is bound to appear inside.

That's where the fallacy is. You can create the pattern in the brain, and if the person does not know about meditation, he may feel a silence, a serenity—for the moment, as long as those waves remain. But you cannot deceive a meditator, because the meditator will see that those patterns are appearing in the brain. The brain is a lower reality, and the lower reality cannot change the higher reality. The mind is the servant; it cannot change the master. But you can experiment. Just remain aware that whether it is a biofeedback machine or a chanting of om, it does not matter; it only creates a mental peace, and a mental peace is not meditation.

Meditation is the flight beyond the mind. It has nothing to do with mental peace.

One of America's great thinkers, Joshua Liebman, has written a very famous book, *Peace of Mind*. I wrote him a letter many years ago when I came across the book, saying that "If you are sincere and honest, you should withdraw the book from the market because there is no such thing as peace of mind. Mind is the problem. When there is no mind, then there is peace, so how can there be peace of mind? And any peace of mind is only fallacious; it simply means the noise has slowed down to such a point that you think it is silence, and you don't have anything to compare it with."

A person who knows what meditation is cannot be deceived by any techniques, because no technique can give you an understanding of the workings of the mind. For example, you feel anger, you feel jealousy, you feel hatred, you feel lust. Is there any technique that can help you to get rid of anger? Of jealousy? Of hatred? Of sexual lust? And if these things remain, your lifestyle is going to remain the same as before. There is only one way—there has never been a second way. There is one and only one way to understand that to be angry is to be stupid: watch anger in all its phases, be alert to it, so it does not catch you unawares. Remain watchful, seeing every step of the anger, and you will be surprised: as awareness about the ways of anger grows, the anger starts evaporating.

And when the anger disappears, then there is a peace. Peace is not a positive achievement. When the hatred disappears, there is love. Love is not a positive achievement. When jealousy disappears, there is a deep friendliness toward all.

Try to understand. . . .

But all the religions have corrupted your minds because they have not taught you how to watch, how to understand. Instead, they have given you conclusions—that "anger is bad." And the moment you condemn something, you have already taken a certain position of judgment. You have judged, and now you cannot be aware. Awareness needs a state of no-judgment, and all the religions have been teaching people judgments: "This is good, this is bad, this is sin, this is virtue." This is the whole crap that man's mind has been loaded with for centuries. So, with everything, the moment you see it, there is immediately a judgment about it within you. You cannot simply see it; you cannot be just a mirror without saying anything.

Understanding arises by becoming a mirror, a mirror of all that goes on in the mind.

There is a beautiful story—not just a story, but an actual historical fact.

One disciple of Gautam Buddha is going on a journey to spread his message. He has come to see Buddha and to get his blessings, and to ask if there is any last message, any last words to be said to him.

Gautam Buddha says, "Just remember one thing: While walking, keep your gaze just four feet ahead, looking four feet ahead of you." Since that day, for twenty-five centuries, Buddhist monks have walked in the same way. That was a strategy to keep you from seeing women in particular. Those disciples were monks, and they had taken the vow of celibacy.

Ananda, another of Gautam Buddha's disciples, could not understand why the monk should keep his eyes always focused four feet ahead. He inquired, "I want to know, what is the reason for it?"

Buddha said, "That's how he will avoid looking at a woman, at least a woman's face—at the most, he will see her feet."

"But," Ananda said, "there may be situations when a woman is in a danger. For example, she has fallen into a well and is shouting for help. What is your disciple supposed to do? He will have to see her face, her body."

Buddha said, "In special situations, he is allowed to see her, but it is not the rule, it is only the exception."

Ananda said, "What about touching?—because there may be situations when a woman has fallen on the road. What is your disciple supposed to do? Should he help her to get up or not? Or an old woman wants to cross the road—what is your disciple supposed to do?"

Buddha said, "As an exception—but remember it is not a rule—he can touch the woman with one condition, and if he cannot fulfill the condition, he is not allowed the exceptions. The condition is that he should remain just a mirror, he should not take any judgment, any attitude. 'The woman is beautiful'—that is a judgment. 'The woman is fair'—that is a judgment. He should remain a mirror, then he is allowed the exceptions. Otherwise, let the woman stay in the well; somebody else will save her. You save yourself!"

What he is saying is that in every situation where the mind starts any kind of desire, greed, lust, ambition, possessiveness, the meditator has to be just a mirror. And what is that going to do? To be just a mirror means you are simply aware. In pure awareness the mind cannot drag you down into the mud, into the gutter. In anger, in hatred, in jealousy, the mind is absolutely impotent in the face of awareness. And because the mind is absolutely impotent, your whole being is in a profound silence—the peace that passeth understanding.

Naturally that peace, that silence, that joy, that blissfulness will affect the brain. It will create ripples in the brain, it will change the wavelengths in the brain, and the scientist will be reading those wave patterns and he will be thinking, *If these wave patterns can be created in someone using mechanical devices, then we will be able to create the profoundness of a Gautam Buddha.*

Don't be stupid.

All your technical devices can be good, can be helpful. They are not going to do any harm; they will be giving you some taste of peace, of silence—although very superficial, still it is something for those who have never known anything of peace. For the thirsty, even dirty water does not look dirty. For the thirsty, even dirty water is a great blessing.

So you can experiment, but remember it is not meditation; it is a little rest, a little relaxation, and there is nothing wrong in it. But if people get the idea that this is meditation, then it is certainly harmful—because these people will stop at the technical things, with the superficial silence, thinking that this is all and they have gained it.

These machines can be helpful to people. But they should be told, "This is just a mechanical way of putting your mind at peace, and the mind at peace is not the real peace—real peace is when mind is absent. That is not possible from the outside, but only from the inside. And inside, you have the intelligence, the understanding to do the miracle."

It is good for people who cannot relax, who cannot find a few moments of peace, whose minds are continuously chattering—these technical devices are good, the biofeedback mechanisms are good. But it should be clear to them that this is not meditation, this is just a mechanical device to help people relax, to give a superficial feeling of silence. If this silence creates an urge to find the real, the inner, the authentic source of peace, then those technical devices have been friends, and the technicians who have been using them have not been barriers but have been bridges.

So give people the little taste that is possible through machines, but don't give them the false idea that this is what meditation is. Tell them that this is only a faraway echo of the real; if you want the real, you will have to go through a deep inner search, a profound understanding of your mind, an awareness of all the cunning ways of the mind so that the mind can be put aside. Then the mind is no longer between you and existence, and the doors are open.

Meditation is the ultimate experience of blissfulness. It cannot be produced by drugs, it cannot be produced by machines, it cannot be produced from the outside.

Self, No-Self, and Reincarnation

As far as I am concerned, not a single word from me has to be believed, but to be experienced. And I am giving you the method, how to experience it.

Become more meditative. Reincarnation and God, heaven and hell do not matter. What matters is your becoming alert. Meditation awakens you, gives you eyes—and then whatever you see, you cannot deny.

To me it seems that the Christian concept of the soul is the same as what you mean by the one who is the watcher. Why didn't Jesus speak about the possibility of reincarnation of the soul? This seems to be a difference between Eastern and Western religions. Can you say something about it?

Jesus knew perfectly well about reincarnation.

There are indirect hints spread all over the Gospels. Just the other day I was saying, quoting Jesus: "I am before Abraham ever was." And Jesus says, "I will be coming back." There are a thousand and one indirect references to reincarnation. He knew about it perfectly well, but there is some other reason why he did not talk about it, why he did not preach it.

Jesus had been to India, and he had seen what happened because of the theory of reincarnation. In India, for almost five thousand years before Jesus, the theory was taught. And it is a truth, it is not only a theory; the theory is based in truth. Man has millions of lives. It was taught by Mahavira, by Buddha, by Krishna, by Rama; all the Indian religions agree upon it. You will be surprised to know that they don't agree on anything else except this theory.

Hindus believe in God and the soul. Jainas don't believe in God at all, but only in the soul. And Buddhists don't believe in the soul or God either. But about reincarnation, all three agree—even Buddhists agree, who don't believe in the soul. A very strange thing ... then who reincarnates? Even the Buddhists could not deny the phenomenon of reincarnation, although they could deny the existence of the soul; they say the soul does not exist but reincarnation exists. And it was very difficult for them to prove reincarnation without the soul; it seems almost impossible. But they found a way—of course, it is very subtle and very difficult to comprehend, but they seem to be closer, the closest to the truth.

It is easy to understand that there is a soul and when you die the body is left on the earth and the soul enters into another body, into another womb; it is a simple, logical, mathematical thing. But Buddha says there is no soul, only a continuum. It is like when you light a candle in the evening and in the morning when you are blowing it out—a question can be asked of you: Are you blowing out the same light that you kindled in the evening? No, it is not the same light, and yet a continuity is there. In the night when you lit the candle . . . that flame is no longer there, that flame is continually disappearing and being replaced by another flame. The replacement is so quick that you can't see the gaps, but with sophisticated scientific instruments, it is possible to see the gaps: one flame going out, another coming up, that going out, another coming up. There are bound to be small intervals, but you can't see them with the naked eye.

Buddha says that just as the candle flame is not the same—it is changing constantly, although in another sense it is the same because it is the same continuum—exactly like that, there is no soul entity in you like a thing, but one like a flame. It is continually changing; it is a river.

Buddha does not believe in nouns, he believes only in verbs, and I perfectly agree with him. He has come closest to the truth; at least in his expression, he is the most profound.

But why did Jesus, Moses, Mohammed—the sources of all the three religions that have been born outside India—not talk about reincarnation directly? For a certain reason, and the reason is that Moses was aware . . . because Egypt and India have been in constant contact. It is suspected that once Africa was part of Asia and that the continent has slowly shifted away. India and Egypt were joined together, hence there are so many similarities. And it is not strange that South India is black; it has partly Negro blood in its veins, it is negroid—not totally, but if Africa was joined with Asia, then certainly the mingling of the Aryans with the Negroes must have happened, and then South India became black.

Moses must have been perfectly aware of India. You will be surprised that Kashmir claims that both Moses and Jesus are buried there. The tombs are there—one tomb for Moses and one tomb for Jesus.

Moses and Jesus saw what happened to India through the theory of reincarnation. Because of the theory of reincarnation, India became very lethargic: there is no hurry. India has no time sense, not even now. Even though everybody is wearing a wristwatch, there is no time sense. If somebody says, "I will be coming at five o'clock in the evening to see you," it can mean anything. He may turn up at four, he may turn up at six, he may not turn up at all— and it is not taken seriously! It is not that he is not fulfilling his promise, but that there is no time sense! How can you have time sense when eternity is available? When there are so many lives, why be in such a hurry? One can go on slowly; one is bound to reach some day or other.

The theory of reincarnation made India very lethargic, dull. It made India utterly time-unconscious. It helped people to postpone. And if you can postpone for tomorrow, then today you will remain the same as you have been, and the tomorrow never comes. And India knows how to postpone not only to tomorrow but even to the next life.

Moses and Jesus both visited India, both were aware. Mohammed never visited India but was perfectly aware, because he was very close to India and there was constant traffic between India and Arabia. They decided that it was better to tell people, "There is only one life, this is the last chance—the first and the last—if you miss it, you miss forever." This is a device to create intense longing, to create such intensity in people that they can be transformed easily.

Then the question arises: Were Mahavira, Buddha, and Krishna not aware? Were they not aware that this theory of reincarnation would create lethargy? They were trying a totally different device. And each device has its time; once it is used, it cannot go on being used forever. People become accustomed to it.

When Buddha, Mahavira, and Krishna tried the device of reincarnation, they were trying it from a totally different angle. India was a very rich country in those days. It was thought to be the golden country of the world, the richest. And in a rich country, the real problem, the greatest problem, is boredom. That is happening now in the West, and all the Westernized countries are in the same situation. Boredom has become the greatest problem. People are utterly bored, so bored that they would like to die.

Krishna, Mahavira, and Buddha used this situation. They told people, "This is nothing, one life's boredom is nothing. You have lived for many lives—and remember, if you don't listen, you are going to live many more lives; you will be bored again and again and again. It is the same wheel of life and death that keeps on moving."

They painted boredom in such dark colors that people who were already bored with even one life became really very deeply involved with religion. One has to get rid of life and death; one has to get out of this wheel, this vicious circle of birth and death. Hence it was relevant in those days.

Then India became poor. Once the country became poor, boredom disappeared. A poor man is never bored, remember; only a rich man can afford boredom, it is a rich man's privilege. It is impossible for a poor man to feel boredom; he has no time. The whole day he is working; when he comes home, he is so tired, he falls asleep. He need not have many entertainments—television and movies and music and art and museums—he need not have all these things, he *cannot* have them. His only entertainment is sex: a natural thing, inbuilt. That's why poor countries go on reproducing more children than rich countries—sex is the only entertainment.

If you want to reduce the population of poor countries, give them more entertainment. Give them television sets, give them radios, movies—something that can keep them distracted from sex.

I have heard about American couples that they become so obsessed with the television that even while making love, they go on watching it. Lovemaking becomes secondary; television becomes primary. They don't want to miss the program that is going on.

A poor country knows only one entertainment because it cannot afford any other; it can afford only the natural, inbuilt one. So a poor country goes on producing people; it becomes more and more crowded. And they are not fed up with life. What life do they have? First you have to have life to be fed up with it. You have to have money to be fed up with it. You have to have many women to be fed up with them. You have to have many experiences of the world to be finished with it.

The moment India became poor, the theory of reincarnation became an escape, a hope—rather than a boredom, it became a hope, a possibility to postpone. "I am poor in this life. Nothing to be worried about; there are many lives. Next life, I am going to strive a little harder and I will be richer. This life, I have got an ugly woman. Nothing to be worried about; it is only a question of one life. Next time I am not going to make the same mistake again. This time I am suffering from my past karmas. This life I will not commit any wrong things so that I can enjoy the coming life." It became a way of postponement.

Jesus saw it, that the device was no longer working in the way it was meant to work. The situation had changed. Now Jesus had to create another device: there is only one life—so if you want to be religious, if you want to meditate, if you want to become a seeker, be one *right now*—because the tomorrow is not reliable. There may be no tomorrow.

Hence the West has become too conscious of time; everybody is in a hurry. This hurry is because of Christianity. The device has again failed. No device can work forever.

My own experience is that a particular device works only while the master is alive, because he is the soul of it—he manages it in such a way that it works. Once the master is gone, the device falls out of use or people start finding new interpretations for it.

Now in the West, the device has failed utterly; now it has become a problem. People are in a constant hurry, tension, anxiety, because there is only one life. Jesus wanted them to remember: Because there is one life, remember God. And what are they doing? Seeing that there is only one life, they want to drink, eat, and be merry, because there is no other life. So indulge as much as you can. Squeeze the whole juice of life right now! And who cares about what will happen on the Judgment Day? Who knows whether the Judgment Day exists or not?

A great hurry has arisen in the West about everything, because there is no other life.

Mary and John are both living in a big apartment building in New York City. One day they meet and instantly fall in love with each other, but they don't make any contact. This goes on for six months until John just can't bear the tension anymore and asks her to come to his apartment for a drink. Hesitatingly she says yes, and as soon as they reach his flat, they close the door behind them and rush into the bedroom and throw themselves on the bed.

After a few minutes, John explains with a hoarse voice, "Listen, I am very sorry, but if I had known that you were a virgin, I would have taken more time."

Mary replies, "Well, if I had known that you had more time, I would have taken my pants off!"

Such a hurry! Speed is the mania, faster and faster. Nobody is bothered where you are going, but you have to go fast, invent speedier vehicles.

And this whole thing has happened because of the device. It worked in Jesus' time. He was continually telling his people, "Beware! The Day of Judgment is very close by. You are going to see the end of the world in your very own life, and there is no other life. And if you miss, you will be thrown into hell for eternity!" He was simply creating a psychological atmosphere. It worked when he was alive and it worked for a few more days when he was gone. It continued to work for a few days because of the closest disciples who had something of the climate of Jesus with them, some aura, but then it created just the opposite effect.

It has created the most worldly civilization the world has ever known. And the desire was that the idea of one life would make people so alert and aware that they would seek and search for God and they would drop all other desires and all other occupations.

Their whole life would become one—pointedly an inquiry, a search for God. That was the idea behind the device. But the ultimate result is that people have become absolutely worldly, because there is no other life, only one life—enjoy it the most you can! Enjoy it; don't postpone it for tomorrow.

The Indian device failed because people became lethargic. It worked with Buddha. He really created one of the greatest movements in the world. Thousands of people renounced their lives, became *sannyasins*. That means they devoted their whole energy to the search for truth, because he created such an atmosphere of boredom that you would be bored if you missed.

But what happened later on was just the opposite. It is always going to be so. The masters are bound to be misunderstood. And people are so cunning, so diplomatic, they can always find ways to destroy the whole device.

Jesus knows perfectly that life is eternal, reincarnation is a fact. He mentions it in indirect ways, maybe to his very close disciples he mentions it, but not to the masses—for a simple reason: he has seen that it failed in India, so something else has to be tried.

I am creating many devices because others have failed. I know perfectly well that my devices will function only while I am here; they are bound to fail as every other device has failed. I am not living in any fool's paradise thinking that my devices will remain as I create them forever. When I am not there, people are going to distort them. But that is natural, it has to be accepted; there is nothing to worry about.

Hence those who are here, please be alert and use these devices as deeply as possible. While I am here, these devices will function perfectly well. In my hands, they can be great situations for inner transformation, but once my hands are no longer visible, these same devices will be in the hands of the pundits and the scholars, and then the same story will be repeated as it has been in the past. Beware, be watchful. Don't waste time.

A friend, who has a Ph.D. in computing, and whose thesis was on artificial intelligence, says that man is a biochemical computer and nothing more. Buddha has said that all things are composite and there is no self, no soul, no spirit, no "I," which seems to agree with my friend's viewpoint. Could you please help me, because I feel that there is something missing from these views, but I can't see it myself.

Man certainly is a biocomputer—but something more, too.

About most people, it can be said that they are only biocomputers and nothing more. Ordinarily one is only the body and the mind, and both are composites. Unless one moves into meditation, one cannot find that which is something more, something transcendental to body and mind.

The psychologists, particularly the behaviorists, have been studying man for half a century, but they study the ordinary man, and of course their thesis is proved by all their studies. The ordinary man, the unconscious man, has nothing more in him than the body–mind composite. The body is the outer side of the mind, and the mind is the inner side of the body. Both are born and both will die one day.

But there is something more. That "something more" makes a person awakened, enlightened, a Buddha, a Christ. But a Buddha or a Christ is not available to be studied by Pavlov, Skinner, Delgado, and others. Their study is about the unconscious man, and of course, when you study the unconscious man, you will not find anything transcendental in him. The transcendental exists in the unconscious man only as a potential, as a possibility; it is not yet realized; it is not yet a reality. Hence you cannot study it.

You can study it only in a Buddha—but even then, study is obviously very difficult, close to impossible, because what you will study in a Buddha will again be his behavior. If you are determined that there is nothing more, if you have already concluded, then even in his behavior you will see only mechanical reactions; you will not see his spontaneity. To see that spontaneity, you have also to become a participant in meditation.

Psychology can become only a real psychology when meditation becomes its foundation. The word *psychology* means "the science of the soul." Modern psychology is not yet a science of the soul.

Buddha certainly has denied the self, the ego, the "I." He has not denied the soul, and the self and the soul are not synonymous. He denies the self because the self exists only in the unconscious man. The unconscious man needs a certain idea of "I"; otherwise he will be without a center. He does not know his real center. He has to invent a false center so that he can at least function in the world; otherwise his functioning will become impossible. He needs a certain idea of "I."

You must have heard about Descartes's famous statement: *Cogito, ergo sum.* "I think, therefore I am."

A professor, teaching the philosophy of Descartes, was asked by a student, "Sir, I think, but how do I know that I am?"

The professor pretended to peer around the classroom. "Who is asking the question?" he said.

"I am," replied the student.

One needs a certain idea of "I"; otherwise functioning will become impossible. So because we don't know the real "I," we substitute it with a false "I"—something invented, a composite.

Buddha denies the self because to him "self" simply is another name for the ego with a little color of spirituality; otherwise there is no difference. His word is *anatta*. *Atta* means "self," *anatta* means "no-self." But he is not denying the soul. In fact, when the self is completely dropped, only then will you come to know the soul. But Buddha does not say anything about it, because nothing can be said.

His approach is *via negativa*. He says: You are not the body, you are not the mind, you are not the self. He goes on denying, eliminating; he eliminates everything that you can conceive of, and then he does not say anything about what is left. That which is left is your reality—that utterly pure sky without clouds, no thought, no identity, no emotion, no desire, no ego, nothing is left. All clouds have disappeared . . . just the pure sky.

It is inexpressible, unnamable, indefinable. That's why he keeps absolutely silent about it. He knows that if anything is said about it, you will immediately jump back to your old idea of the self. If he says, "There is a soul in you," what are you going to understand? You will think, "He calls it soul and we call it self—it is the same. The supreme self maybe, the spiritual self; it is not just ordinary ego." But spiritual or unspiritual, the idea of being a separate entity is the point. Buddha denies that you are a separate entity from the whole. You are one with the organic unity of existence, so there is no need to say anything about your separateness. Even the word *soul* will give you a certain idea of separateness; you are bound to understand it in your own unconscious way.

Your friend says that man is a biochemical computer and nothing more—can a biochemical computer say that? Can a biochemical computer deny the self, the soul? No biocomputer or any other kind of computer has any idea of self or no-self. But your friend is doing that, so certainly he is not a biochemical computer. No biochemical computer can write a thesis on artificial intelligence! Do you think artificial intelligence can write a thesis about artificial intelligence? Something more is needed.

Is it wrong to think that Buddha agrees with his viewpoint? Not at all. Buddha's experience is of meditation. Without meditation, nobody can have any idea what Buddha is talking about. Your friend's observation is from the standpoint of a scientific onlooker: it is not his experience; it is his observation. He is studying biochemical computers, artificial intelligence, from the outside. Who is studying?

Can you conceive of two computers studying each other? The computer can know only that which has been fed into it; it cannot have more than that. The information has to be given to it, then it keeps it in its memory—it is a memory system. It can do miracles as far as mathematics is concerned. A computer can be far more efficient than any Albert Einstein as far as mathematics is concerned, but a computer cannot be a meditator. Can you imagine a computer just sitting silently doing nothing, the spring comes and the grass grows by itself? . . .

There are many qualities that are impossible for the computer. A computer cannot be in love. You can keep many computers together—they will not fall in love! A computer cannot have any experience of beauty; a computer cannot know any bliss. A computer cannot have any awareness. A computer is incapable of feeling silence. These are the qualities that prove that man has something more than artificial intelligence.

Artificial intelligence can do scientific work, mathematical work, calculation—and very quickly and efficiently, because it is a machine. But a machine cannot be aware of what it is doing. A computer cannot feel boredom, a computer cannot feel meaninglessness, a computer cannot experience anguish. A computer cannot start an inquiry about truth, it cannot renounce the world and become a seeker, it cannot go to the mountains or to the monasteries. It cannot conceive of anything beyond the mechanical—and all that is significant is beyond the mechanical.

How can one distinguish between enlightened self-love and egomania?

The distinction is subtle but very clear, not difficult. If you have egomania, it will create more and more misery for you. Misery will indicate that you are ill. Egomania is a disease, a cancer of the soul. Egomania will make you more and more tense, will make you more and more uptight, will not allow you to relax at all. It will drive you toward insanity.

Self-love is just the opposite of egomania. In self-love there is no self, only love. In egomania there is no love, only self. In self-love you will start becoming more and more relaxed. A person who loves himself is totally relaxed. To love somebody else may create a little tension, because the other need not be always in tune with you. The other may have his or her own ideas. The other is a different world; there is every possibility of collision, clash. There is every possibility of storm and thunder because the other is a different world. There is always a subtle struggle going on. But when you love yourself, there is nobody else. There is no conflict—it is pure silence, it is tremendous delight. You are alone; nobody disturbs you. The other is not needed at all. And to me, a person who has become capable of such deep love toward himself becomes capable of loving others. If you cannot love yourself, how can you love others? It must first happen at close quarters, it must first happen within you, to spread toward others.

People try to love others, not being at all aware that they have not even loved themselves. How can you love others? That which you don't have you cannot share. You can give to others only that which you have already with you.

So the first and the most basic step toward love is love of oneself; but it has no self in it.

Let me explain it to you.

The "I" arises only as a contrast to the "thou." "I" and "thou" exist together. The "I" can exist in two dimensions. One dimension is "I–it": you—your house, you—your car, you—your money; "I–it." When there is this "I," this "I" of "I–it," your "I" is almost like a thing. It is not consciousness; it is fast asleep, snoring. Your consciousness is not there. You are just like things, a thing amidst things: part of your house, part of your furniture, part of your money.

Have you watched it? A man who is too greedy about money, by and by starts having the qualities of money. He becomes just money. He loses spirituality; he is no more a spirit. He is reduced to a thing. If you love money, you will become like money. If you love your house, by and by you will become material. Whatsoever you love, you become. Love is alchemical. Never love the wrong thing, because it will transform you. Nothing is so transforming as love. Love something that can raise you higher, to higher altitudes. Love something beyond you.

That is the whole effect of religion: to give you a love object like God so that there is no way to fall down. One has to rise.

One sort of "I" exists as "I–it;" another sort of "I" exists as "I–thou." When you love a person, another type of "I" arises in you: "I–thou." You love a person; you become a person.

But what about self-love?—there is no "it" and there is no "thou." "I" disappears because "I" can exist only in two contexts: "it" and "thou." "I" is the figure, "it" and "thou" function as the field. When the field disappears, the "I" disappears. When you are left alone, you are, but you don't have an "I," you don't feel any "I." You are simply a deep *amness*. Ordinarily we say "I am." In that state, when you are deep in love with yourself, "I" disappears. Only amness, pure existence, pure being remains. It will fill you with tremendous bliss. It will make you a celebration, a rejoicing. There will be no problem in distinguishing between them.

If you are getting more and more miserable, then you are on the trip of being an egomaniac. If you are becoming more and more tranquil, silent, happy, together, then you are on another trip—the trip of self-love. If you are on the trip of ego, you will become destructive to others—because the ego tries to destroy the "thou." If you are moving toward self-love, the ego will disappear. And when the ego disappears, you allow the other to be himself or herself; you give total freedom. If you don't have any ego, you cannot create an imprisonment for the other you love; you cannot create a cage. You allow the other to be an eagle in the high heavens. You allow the other to be himself or herself; you give total freedom. Love gives total freedom. Love *is* freedom—freedom for you and freedom for the object of your love. Ego is bondage—bondage for you and bondage for your victim.

But ego can play very deep tricks with you. It is very cunning, and subtle are its ways: it can pretend to be self-love.

Let me tell you one anecdote.

Mulla Nasruddin's face lit up as he recognized the man who was walking ahead of him down the subway stairs. He slapped the man so heartily on the back that the man nearly collapsed, and cried, "Goldberg, I hardly recognized you! Why, you have gained thirty pounds since I saw you last. And you have had your nose fixed, and I swear you are about two feet taller."

The man looked at him angrily. "I beg your pardon," he said in icy tones, "but I do not happen to be Goldberg."

"Aha!" said Mulla Nasruddin, "so you have even changed your name?"

The ego is very cunning and very self-justifying, very self-rationalizing. If you are not very alert, it can start hiding itself behind self-love. The very word *self* will become a protection for it. It can say, "I am your self." It can change its weight, it can change its height, it can change its name. And because it is just an idea, there is no problem about it: it can become small; it can become big. It is just your fantasy.

Be very careful. If you really want to grow in love, much carefulness will be needed. Each step has to be taken in deep alertness so ego cannot find any loophole to hide behind.

Your real self is neither I nor thou; it is neither you nor the other. Your real self is altogether transcendental. What you call "I" is not your real self. "I" is imposed on reality. When you call somebody "you," you are not addressing the real self of the other. Again you have imposed a label on it. When all the labels are taken away, the real self remains—and the real self is as much yours as it is others'. The real self is one.

That's why we go on saying that we participate in each other's beings, we are members of each other. Our real reality is God. We may be like icebergs floating in the ocean—they appear to be separate—but once we melt, nothing will be left. Definition will disappear, limitation will disappear, and the iceberg will not be there. It will become part of the ocean.

The ego is an iceberg. Melt it. Melt it in deep love, so it disappears and you become part of the ocean.

I have heard. . . .

The judge looked very severe. "Mulla," he said, "your wife says you hit her over the head with a baseball bat and threw her down a flight of stairs. What have you got to say for yourself?"

Mulla Nasruddin rubbed the side of his nose with his hand, and meditated. Finally he said, "Your Honor, I guess there are three sides to this case: my wife's story, my story, and the truth."

Yes, he is perfectly right.

"You have heard about two sides of a truth," he said, "but there are three sides"—and he is exactly right. There is your story, my story, and the truth; I and you and the truth.

The truth is neither I nor you. I and you are an imposition on the vastness of the truth. "I" is false, "you" is false; utilitarian, useful in the world. It will be difficult to manage the world without "I" and "you." Good—use them, but they are just devices of the world. In reality, there is neither "you" nor "I." Something, someone, some energy exists with no limitations, with no boundaries. Out of it we come, and into it we disappear again.

I have heard you say that Buddha would not speak of God, because it cannot be proved. Yet in the next breath, he speaks of other lives, and reincarnation. How does this fit into scientific fact?

Buddha says there is no soul. What is it that remains after death? What is reincarnation? I vaguely understand that it can be the formless that remains, but can that have an individual entity? The same wave is not reborn.

The question is very significant. It is one of the most fundamental contributions of Buddha to human consciousness—the idea of no-self. It is very complex. You will have to be very silently alert to understand it, because it goes against all the patterns that you have been conditioned to.

First a few analogies, so you have a certain idea what he means by no-self. Your body is a bag of skin. The skin defines your body; it defines where you and the world start. It is a demarcation around you. It protects you from the world, it divides you from the world, and it allows you only certain apertures to enter into the world or let the world enter in you. If there is no skin, you will not be able to exist. You will be losing your boundaries with all that surrounds you. But you are not your skin. And skin goes on changing.

It is just like the snake who goes on getting out of his old skin again and again. You also get out of your skin again and again many times. If you ask the physiologists, they will say that if a man is going to live seventy years, then nearly ten times he will change his skin completely. But the process is very slow, so you never become aware of it. Such a tiny part changes every moment that you cannot feel it; your senses are not so subtle. The change is very subtle. The skin goes on changing and still you go on thinking to yourself that this is your body, the same body. It is not the same body; it is a continuum.

When you were in your mother's womb, the first day you were just a small cell, invisible to the naked eye. That was your skin at that time; that was your body. Then you started growing. After nine months, you were born—then you had a totally different body. If suddenly you come across yourself just one day old, just born, you will not be able to recognize that this is you. You have changed so much. But still you think you are the same. In a way you are the same because you are the same continuity. In a way you are not the same, because you have been continually changing.

In the same way, just like the skin, is the ego. The skin holds your body into a pattern, into a definition, into a limit. The ego holds the contents of your mind into a limit. The ego is the inner skin so that you know who you are; otherwise you will be lost— you will not know who is who; who is me and who is the other.

The idea of self, I, ego, gives you a definition, a utilitarian definition. It makes you clearly separate from others. But that, too, is a skin, a very subtle skin, that holds all the contents of your mind— your memory, your past, your desires, your plans, your future, your present, your love, your hate, anger, sadness, happiness—it holds all that in a bag. But you are not that ego either. Because that, too, goes on changing, and that changes more than the bodily skin. Each moment it is changing.

Buddha uses the analogy of a flame. A lamp is lighted: you see the flame, but it is perpetually changing: it is never the same. By the morning when you put the light off, you don't put the same flame off. It has been continually changing the whole night.

Every single moment the flame is disappearing in the smoke and the new flame is replacing it. But the replacement is so fast that you cannot see the absence—that one flame has gone, another has come. That is gone; another has come. The movement is so fast that you cannot see the gap between the two. Otherwise there is only a continuity; it is not the same flame. But still, in a way, it is the same flame because it is the continuity of the same flame. It is born out of the same flame.

Just as you were born out of your parents—you are a continuity. You are not the same. You are not your father, you are not your mother—but still you are your father and your mother, because you continue the same tradition, the same line, the same heritage.

Buddha says the ego is a continuity, it is not a substance— continuity like a flame, continuity like a river, continuity like the body.

The problem arises . . . we can concede that okay, it may be so: if a person dies at death and everything disappears, then perfectly true, maybe it is just a flame. But Buddha says a person is reborn— then the problem arises. Then who is reborn?

Then again, a few analogies. Have you seen a big house on fire, or a jungle on fire? If you watch, you will come to see a phenomenon. The flame simply jumps from one tree and reaches another tree. It has no substance in it: it is just a flame. It has no material in it, it is just pure energy, a certain quantity of energy—it jumps from one tree and reaches the other and the other is on fire.

Or, you can bring an unlighted torch close to a lighted torch. What happens? The flame from the lighted torch jumps to the unlighted torch. It is a quantum leap; it is a jump. The pure flame jumps toward the other torch and starts another continuity.

Or, right now you are listening to me. If you put a radio on, suddenly you will start listening to a certain broadcast from some station that is passing through the air right now. Just a receiver is needed. Once a receiver is there, you can catch hold of something that is being broadcast from London or from Moscow or Beijing.

No substance is coming, just pure thought waves jumping from Beijing to Pune ... just thought waves, nothing substantial. You cannot hold them in your hand, you cannot see them, but they are there because your radio set catches them, or your television catches them.

Buddha says when a person dies, his whole life's accumulated desires, his whole life's accumulated memories, his whole life's patterns, karmas, jump like energy waves into a new womb. It is a jump. The exact word exists in physics: they call it *quantum leap*—a leap of pure energy without any substance in it.

Buddha is the first quantum physicist. Einstein followed him after twenty-five centuries, but they both speak the same language. And I still say that Buddha is scientific. His language is of modern physics; he came twenty-five centuries before his time.

When a person dies, the body disappears, the material part

disappears, but the immaterial part, the mind part, is a vibration. That vibration is released, broadcast. Now, wherever a right womb is ready for this vibe, it will enter into the womb.

There is no "self" going—there is nobody going, there is no ego going. There is no need for anything substantial to go, it is just a push of energy. The emphasis is that it is again the same bag of the ego jumping. One house has become unlivable, one body is no longer possible to live with. The old desire, the lust for life— Buddha's term is *tanha*, "lust for life"—is alive, burning. That very desire takes a jump.

Now, listen to modern physics. They say there is no matter. You see this very substantial wall behind me? You cannot pass through it; if you try, you will be hurt. But modern physics says it is nothing, nothing substantial. It is simply pure energy moving with such tremendous speed that the very movement creates the false illusion, the appearance of substance.

You have sometimes watched a fan moving fast—then you cannot see the blades. There are only three blades, but they are moving so fast, it looks like a solid circle, like a plate; you cannot see the gaps between two blades. If the air blown by a fan is moved with the same velocity as the electrons are moving—the velocity is tremendous—then you could sit on the air and you would not fall from it. You could sit as I am sitting on my chair and you would not feel any movement, because the movement is so fast.

Exactly the same is happening in this chair, and the same is happening beneath you on the floor. It is not a marble floor, that is only an appearance; the energy particles are moving so fast that their very movement, their fastness, creates the illusion of substance.

Substance exists not; only pure energy exists. Modern science says matter exists not; only immaterial energy exists.

Hence I say Buddha is very scientific. He does not talk about God, but he talks about the immaterial no-self. Just as modern science has taken the idea of substance out of its metaphysics, Buddha took the idea of self out of his metaphysics. Self and substance are correlates. It is difficult to believe that the wall is nonsubstantial, and in the same way, it is difficult to believe that no self exists in you.

Now, a few things more, which will make it more clear. I cannot say that you will understand it, but it will make it more clear.

You walk, you are walking, you have gone for a morning walk. The very language—that we say "you are walking"—creates a problem; in our very language is the problem. The moment we say somebody is walking, we assume that somebody is there who is walking—the walker. We ask, how is walking possible if there is no walker?

Buddha says there is no walker, only walking. Life does not consist of things. Buddha says life consists of events. And that is exactly what modern science is saying: there are only processes, not things—events.

Even to say that life exists is not right. Only thousands and thousands of living processes exist. Life is just an idea. There is nothing like "life."

In the sky one day, you see black clouds have gathered and there is thunder and lightning. When there is lightning, do you ask, "Is there something behind lightning? Who is lightning? What is lightning?" No, you will say, "Lightning is simply lightning—there is nobody behind it; it is just a process. It is not that there is something that is lightning. It is simply lightning."

The duality is brought by the language. You are walking—Buddha says there is only walking. You are thinking—Buddha says there is only thinking, no thinker. *Thinker* is just created by the language. Because we use a language that is based in duality, it makes everything into duality.

While you are thinking, there is a cluster of thoughts, all right—but there is no thinker. If you really want to understand it, you will have to meditate deeply and come to a point where thinking disappears. The moment thinking disappears, you will be surprised—the thinker is also gone. With thinking, the thinker also disappears. It was just an appearance of moving thoughts.

You see a river. Does a river really exist, or is it just a movement? If you take the movement out, will there be a river? Once the movement is taken out, the river will disappear. It is not that the river is moving; the river is nothing but rivering.

Language creates the difficulty. Maybe because of this particular structure in certain languages, Buddha became important and significant and became rooted only in Japan, China, Burma—because they have a totally different language. It is very significant to understand why he became so important in the Chinese mind, why China could understand him and India could not. China has a different language, which fits with Buddhist ideology absolutely. The Chinese language does not divide in two. In the Chinese language, or in Korean, or in Japanese or Burmese, a totally different structure exists than in Sanskrit, Hindi, English, Greek, Latin, French, German—a totally different structure.

When for the first time the Bible was being translated into

Burmese, there was much difficulty, because a few sentences could not be translated at all. The moment you translate them, the whole meaning is lost. For example, a simple sentence, "God is"—you cannot translate it into Burmese. If you translate it, it reads "God becomes." "God is" cannot be translated, because there is no equivalent term for *is*—because *is* implies something static.

We can say "the tree is," but in Burmese, you have to say "the tree is becoming," not *is*. There is no equivalent for *is*. The tree *becomes*. By the time you say the tree *is*, it is no longer the same tree, so why do you say *is*? *Is* makes it static. But it is not, it is a river-like phenomenon—"tree is becoming." I have to say "tree is becoming," but in Burmese, it will be simply "tree becoming." The *is* will not be there. "The river is"—if you want to translate, it will be "river moving." "River rivering" will be the exact translation in Burmese.

But to say "God becoming" is very difficult, because Christians cannot say that. God is perfect; he cannot "become." He is not a process, he has no growth possibility—he has already arrived. He is the absolute—what do you mean by *becoming*? Becoming is possible if somebody is imperfect. God is perfect, he cannot become. So how to translate it? Very difficult.

But Buddha immediately penetrated the Burmese, Chinese, Japanese, Korean mind—immediately penetrated. The very structure of their languages made it possible; they could understand Buddha very easily.

In life, there are only events. Eating is there, but there is no eater. Just watch eating. Is there really an eater? You feel hungry, right—hunger is there, but there is nobody who is hungry. Then you eat—eating is there, but there is nobody who is an eater. Then hunger is satisfied, then you feel satiation—this satisfaction is there, but there is nobody who is satisfied.

Buddha says life consists of events. Life means living. Life is not a noun; it is a verb. And everything is a verb. Watch and you will be able to see it: everything is becoming; nothing is static.

Eddington said that in the English language there are a few words that are absolutely false: for example, *rest*. Nothing is ever at rest; the very word is wrong because there is no equivalent in reality. Have you ever seen anything at rest? Even when you are at rest, it is resting, it is not rest. It is a process: something is happening; you are still breathing.

Lying down, relaxing—but it is not rest. Many things, a thousand things are happening. Have you ever seen anything at rest? It is impossible; rest does not exist. Even when a person is dead, then the body continues its processes.

You may not have heard—sometimes it happens: Mohammedans, Christians, those people who bury their dead in the ground, sometimes come to know that the person is dead but his beard has grown, his hair has become longer, his nails have grown. And the person is dead!

Now this is very weird. If you shave a man and put him in the grave and after six months you open the grave and he has a beard . . . now what to say, whether he is alive or dead? You will be very much afraid; you will run back home and that face will haunt you in the night. What has happened? If the man is dead, then how come his beard has grown? And if his beard can grow, is he really dead or not—just pretending?

Life is millions of processes. Even when your ego disappears from this base, takes off from this airport and lands in some other womb, many processes continue still. All processes don't stop, because there are many processes that have nothing to do with your ego. Nothing to do with your ego—your ego can go, and they will continue. Hairs growing, nails growing, have nothing to do with your ego.

And, immediately, the moment your ego leaves, millions of small microbes will become alive and they will start working and functioning. You will be almost like a marketplace! You will be fully alive in that way. Much will be happening: many microbes running, rushing here and there, making love, having marriages, dying, and everything will be happening. The moment you leave the body, your body becomes a landing place for many other people who were waiting, saying, "Please leave! Let us come in."

Life is a continuous process—not only process but *processes*, a continuity.

Buddha says the very idea of self is because of language. You feel hungry: in language we say "I am hungry." Language creates the idea of "I." How to say it? To be exactly right, you can only say "hunger." To say, "I am hungry" is bringing something absolutely false into it. "Hunger"—that's enough.

Watch your processes, and you will feel it. When you feel hungry today, just watch it. Is there really somebody who is hungry or is there just hunger? And is it just a language pattern that gives it a twist and divides it in two, and you start feeling "I am hungry"?

Buddhism is the first religion that brought this message to the world—that your religions, your philosophies, are more grounded in your linguistic patterns than in anything else. And if you can understand your language better, you will be able to understand your inner processes better. He was the first linguist, and his insight is tremendously meaningful.

"You say that Buddha would not speak of God because it cannot be proved. . ."

Yes, he would not speak about God, because it cannot be proved, and he would not speak about God, because the God that you think exists, exists not. Your God is again the same old fallacy of self. You think you have a self, so the whole universe must have a self. Because you have a self, the whole universe must have a *supreme* self. That supreme self is "God."

Buddha says you don't have any self. The universe *is,* but there is no supreme self in it . . . millions of processes, but no supreme self. There is no center to it; it is all circumference.

Very difficult to catch hold of it—unless you meditate. That's why Buddha never goes into metaphysical discussions; he says, "Meditate." Because in meditation these things become so clear. When thinking stops, suddenly you see—the thinker has disappeared. It was a shadow. And when the thinker disappears, how can you say, how can you feel "I am"? There is no "I" left; you are pure space. That's what Buddha calls *anatta,* the pure space of no self. It is a tremendous experience.

". . . yet in the next breath, he speaks of other lives and reincarnation."

He speaks, and Buddhists have always been in trouble because of it. Buddha is so scientific that he cannot twist the facts. If he were not such a scientific man, if he were just a metaphysician, either he would have accepted self to make his whole philosophy look consistent, or he would have dropped the idea of reincarnation, because the two things look contradictory. But he is such a scientist that he will not enforce anything from his mind on reality. He simply stated the fact. If it is contradictory, he says, "Maybe it is contradictory, but it is so."

This is what is happening in modern science. Just fifty years ago, when scientists entered into the innermost core of matter, they were very puzzled, because the electrons were behaving in a very illogical way.

Now you cannot force electrons to be logical, you cannot send them to the university to learn Aristotle, and you cannot tell them, "You are behaving illogically, so behave! This is not correct." You cannot say that. If they are behaving illogically, they are behaving illogically—you have to understand it, that's all; nothing can be done.

And the illogic was really great—it was no ordinary matter. Sometimes the same electron would behave like a wave, and sometimes it would behave like a particle. Now the two things are impossible, they are non-Euclidian and non-Aristotelian—as if these electrons don't believe in Euclid and Aristotle. What are they doing? Have they never heard of Euclid?

It is simply geometry we have all learned in school—that a dot cannot be a line and a line cannot be a dot. A line is many dots put together in sequence, so a single dot cannot behave like a line; otherwise the whole of geometry will be disturbed. You put a dot and you go to the bathroom, you come back and it has become a line! Then what will you do?

But this is exactly what is happening in the innermost core of matter. You go on watching, and it was looking like a dot and suddenly it is a line. And the jump is such that you don't see it even growing into a line. In one instant of time, it is a dot; in another instant of time it is a line—not even growing into a line, just a jump, so sudden, so illogical. If it grew slowly, we could understand that: maybe it is like a seed, sprouting and becoming a tree. Okay, we can understand. In one moment of time it is a seed, in another moment of time it grows, by and by and by and by, gradually, and becomes a tree. We can understand.

If a dot becomes a line slowly, we will be able to understand. But suddenly? And not only suddenly, even more illogical is that two observers in a single moment of time, simultaneously can observe—one can observe it as a dot and another can observe it as a line. Now what to do? One observer is seeing it as a seed and another is seeing it as a tree? In a single moment of time?

The whole of Western science has grown out of Greek logic. And these electrons were rebelling against Aristotle; there was no way to put them right. Scientists tried in many ways, because mind tends to cling to its own concepts, patterns. It is not so easy to relax and surrender to these stupid electrons.

For almost two, three decades, scientists were puzzled and they were trying to find out some way to explain it, or at least to explain it away, why it was happening. But finally they had to concede to the fact and they accepted it. Hence "quantum" physics. We had to find a name for something that was absolutely illogical, and we had no word for it. And when people ask scientists, "How do you explain it? It is illogical," they say, "It is illogical but it is so, and we cannot do anything about it. We have to listen to reality. If reality is illogical, then something must be wrong with our logic, that's all. We can change the logic, but we cannot change the reality."

That's what happened when Buddha came into the world. He entered into the innermost core of your so-called self and he was also puzzled—what to do? There is no self, and there is reincarnation. Now if he were not really such a great scientist, but was just an ordinary philosopher, then he would have forgotten all about it. He would not have talked about this fact at all—he would have chosen. The choice is simple: Either you say there is no reincarnation because there is no self . . .

That's what people who don't believe in the soul have always been saying. The atheists, the materialists, they have always been saying that there is no self—when you die, you simply die. Nothing survives, and there is no rebirth. That's simple, logical. Or there are eternalists, theists, people who believe in the self. They say that you die but only the body dies; your self, your center survives. Your soul, your atman survives; it is eternal. That, too, is logical.

Buddha is very illogical. And he is illogical because his insistence not to go against reality is absolute. His emphasis is this: that whatsoever reality reveals, we have to listen to it. We are not here to impose our own ideologies on it. Who are we to impose? If this is the fact, then something is wrong in our logic, in our language, in our very way of thinking. We have to change that, rather than avoiding, escaping reality. So he seems to be the most absurd thinker in the world, because this is one of the most absurd statements—that you don't exist but you are reborn.

You can see it clearly: it is absurd. If you don't exist, how can you be reborn? And he says, "That I don't know. You don't exist and you are reborn—that much I know, that I have come to see, that I have seen. And if you want to see it, meditate. Go deeper into your being, as I have gone into my being, and you will also be puzzled, very much confused. But by and by you will settle with the reality. And then you will change your whole language."

Buddha changed the whole language, the whole philosophical style. There has never been such an original man before. It was almost impossible to understand him, because he was not speaking the same language as you speak, and he was bringing some new visions into the world.

The person who does not believe in the soul is very old, nothing new in it. Marx is not saying anything new. For thousands of years, there have been atheists who have denied the soul, who have denied rebirth. Neither Mahavira nor Patañjali are saying anything new, because there have always been people who have believed in the soul and reincarnation.

Buddha is bringing a real vision, original. He says there is no soul and yet there is reincarnation. It is a quantum leap.

So when I say that he is a scientist, I mean it. And if you understand the language of modern physics, you will be able to understand Buddha. In fact, to understand Buddha without understanding modern physics is impossible. For the first time, modern physics has provided a parallel. Heisenberg, Planck, and Einstein, they have provided a parallel. Matter has disappeared; there is only energy, with no self in it, no substance in it. And what Buddha says is the same: *anatta*, no self.

"How does this fit into scientific fact?"

It fits perfectly. In fact, when you are asking how it fits into scientific fact, your idea of science is of the nineteenth century; you are not aware of modern science, you are not aware of the latest developments. Your idea of science is orthodox, old, out of date. Science has changed tremendously. If Newton comes back, he will not be able to understand science at all, because science has changed so fast, and its insight has become so puzzling that scientists are speaking like metaphysicians, mystics. They are not talking now like mathematicians; they are talking like mystics and poets.

"I vaguely understand that it can be the formless that remains."

No, you will not be able to understand it intellectually, because your formless will again be of a certain form. How can you conceive the formless? The word is okay, but the moment you try to conceive the formless, immediately it starts taking a form—because only form can be conceived; the formless cannot be conceived. It is an empty word.

You can go on calling God formless, but you cannot conceive it. And whenever even people who talk about a formless God go to worship, they go to worship before a form. Then again there is a statue, a ritual, a god, a goddess, a form. Even a man like Shankara goes on talking about the formless, the attributeless—the *nirguna.* But his worship, his prayer, is of the *saguna*—*with* attribute, *with* form, because it is impossible to conceive the formless. Conception is only of the form. Or, whatsoever you can conceive, by the very possibility of its being conceived, it will take a form. So it is just a vague idea.

You say, *"I vaguely understand that it can be the formless that remains."* No, it is not a question of vaguely comprehending. Intellectually, there is no way. The way is only meditative, existential. You don't figure it out through intellect; you simply move more into meditation, open a new dimension of vision.

Nobody has emphasized meditation as much as Buddha. His whole method is meditation.

And what is meditation? Meditation is, by and by, becoming

thoughtless; not falling into sleep—remaining alert, and yet becoming thoughtless. Once thoughts disappear, everything is crystal clear—that the thinker was just a by-product of moving thoughts. It was a bundle of thoughts and nothing else. It had no separate existence.

Then you walk, but the walker is no more there; then you eat, but the eater is no more there; then you sleep, but the sleeper is no more there; then you live, but there is nobody who is living; then you die, and there is nobody who is dying. You are just a pure space in which millions of processes exist, in which life flows with all its processes and you remain uncorrupted by it. You are like an open sky . . . clouds come and go.

One of the most beautiful names given to Buddha is *tathagata*. It means "thus came, thus gone." There was no one who came and there was no one who has gone—just coming and going. That is the meaning of *tathagata*—just a process of coming and a process of going; there was no one who has come and no one who has gone.

Zen masters have always been saying that this man never existed, this man called Gautam the Buddha never existed. Yes, he came certainly, and he went also, but he never existed. It is just like a dream process. A dream comes and goes, and by the morning you know it never existed.

Once you understand yourself as pure space and many things happening, you become detached. Then you become fearless, because there is nothing to lose, there is nobody to lose anything. Then you are no more full of lust for life, because you don't conceive of any self. Then you are not afraid of death and you are not in a lust for life. Then you don't think of the past and then you don't project the future. Then you simply are—as pure as the vast sky outside;

you also become a pure sky inside. And the meeting of these two skies, the inner and the outer, is what Buddha calls nirvana.

You ask: *"I vaguely understand that it can be the formless that remains, but can that have an individual entity?"*

No, it has no individual entity.

"The same wave is not reborn."

True. In fact, if you watch closely—go to the river or to the ocean and watch waves; you will be surprised to see something new that you never thought of before. When you see a wave coming toward you, nothing is coming, the wave never comes to you. You see it moving toward you; it is not moving. One wave simply helps other waves to arise by the side. The other wave helps another wave to arise. But it happens so fast that it creates a mirage, an illusion—you think the same wave is coming toward you. Nothing is coming toward you.

When one wave arises, by the impact of that wave, other waves arise; just in the close vicinity, another wave. By the force of the first wave, second wave; by the force of the second wave, third wave; by the force of the third, the fourth—that's how waves arise. But they give an illusion as if the same wave is coming toward you. They never come. When you see a wave arising far away there on the horizon, it remains there; it never comes to you.

It can happen: you can put a piece of driftwood just in the middle of the river: that driftwood will come to you, but don't be deceived by it—the wave is not coming. When one wave goes high, that driftwood moves to the other wave; the other wave goes high, it moves with the third wave. With the rising and falling waves, the driftwood comes to the shore, but the waves never come. This is a scientific fact. They only appear to be reaching.

Right, precisely, that is what Buddha is saying: *The same wave is not reborn.* He is not saying you will be reborn, he simply says there is a rebirth.

But in a way we can say you will be born, because it will be a continuity. The same wave: wave A creates wave B, wave B creates wave C—it is a continuity; a continuum is the right word. That, too, comes from modern physics: continuum.

Buddha calls it *santati.* Just as a child is born to you: he is you in a certain way, and yet not you, not totally you. He will have his own personality, but you created the wave. It is father's and mother's energy creating a new wave. This wave will go—the father may die, the mother may die—this wave will continue, and this wave will create other waves in its own way, in its own time.

Santati, continuum. You are not born, only your desires are born again; because you are not, so you cannot be born. Hence, Buddha says, if you drop desiring, you will never be born again. Hence, if you understand the whole futility of desire and you stop desiring, you drop desiring, then there will be no birth for you.

Then, first you become a *srotapanna,* you enter into the stream, you start understanding how things are, what things are: life processes with no self. This is what he means by becoming a *srotapanna,* entering the stream: entering into the idea of the stream—that life is like a river, not static but dynamic; no things but only events; a dynamism, an energy phenomenon.

Then, by and by, as you move deeper into this stream you become a *skridagamin*—only once more will you be born. You understand, but yet your understanding is not total. Then you become an *anagamin*—you will not be born again. You have understood the whole phenomenon. In that very understanding you are liberated.

By becoming capable of not being born again, you become an *arhat*—one who has achieved, one who has arrived. Now I am using a language that is not Buddhist, so beware. I have to use a language that is not Buddhist, so I am using terms—I say, "one has arrived." Now, there is no other way to say it, but you have to understand: when I say one has arrived, there is no "one," only arrival... only *arriving*, not even "arrival."

Buddha's vision is very existential, and nothing is as liberating as Buddha's vision. Because if you believe in a soul, you can leave the world, but then you will desire paradise—because you don't leave your self. Desire shifts into a new dimension. You drop greed, but really you don't drop it—subtle greed arises.

Just see the paradise of Mohammedans or Christians or Hindus. It looks so worldly, so profane. Because whatsoever these religions are telling you to drop here is provided there—and in bulk! They say, "Don't drink alcohol!" and in the Mohammedan paradise, *phirdous*, rivers of alcohol are there. There is no need to purchase or buy it, there is no need to carry a license; you just jump in. You can bathe in it; you can swim in it. Now, what is this?

In Mohammedan countries, homosexuality has been so prevalent that even that is provided for. Not only beautiful women are there, but beautiful boys are also provided. Now this looks ugly, but it is the ordinary human mind....

Whatsoever you are dropping here, you are dropping only in order to get more—this is the logic. Beautiful women—*apsaras* Hindus call them, *houris* Mohammedans call them... and not only *houris* but *gilmis*, beautiful boys, handsome boys also are available, because a few homosexuals will reach heaven and what will they do?

Buddha says unless you drop the self, you will go on perpetuating the same nonsense again and again. Your paradise will be nothing but a projected world—the same world modified, made more beautiful, more decorated. Here on the earth, women age, become old. In paradise, in the Hindu paradise, they never become old; they are stuck at the age of sixteen. They must be feeling so fed up—stuck at the age of sixteen; they never grow beyond that.

In fact, that is the desire of every woman—to get stuck at sixteen. It never happens here, but it happens "there".... After sixteen, women grow very reluctantly: their birthday comes only once every three or four years. But that has been the desire, to make beauty permanent. Here it is impossible. Even with all the scientific gadgets, instruments, potions, plastic surgery, this and that, even then it is not possible. One has to age. In paradise—Hindu, Mohammedan, Christian, Jewish—that miracle has happened! God has prepared a beautiful walled garden paradise for you. He is waiting. If you are virtuous, if you obey him, you will be rewarded tremendously; if you disobey, then hell. So the self exists here as the center of desire, and God exists as the center of fulfilling that desire.

Buddha says both are not, get rid of both; neither God exists, nor self. Look at reality, don't move in desires. Drop fantasies, stop dreaming, and look at what is. And he says there is only this impermanent world of processes—this fluxlike world, this vortex of reality ... everything impermanent and changing, nothing is permanent.

That is the meaning of his insistence that there is no self, because you are trying to make something in you permanent. You say, "The body changes, okay; the world changes, okay; relationships change, become rotten, okay—but the self, the self is eternal. Yes, this visible world changes—but the invisible god, he is eternal." You want something eternal so desperately that you start believing in it. It is your desire that the eternal should be there.

Buddha says there is nothing eternal. Everything is impermanent; everything is in flow. Understand this, and this very understanding will liberate you.

Remember, when others talk of liberation, they talk of liberation for the self. When Buddha talks of liberation, he talks of liberation *from* the self. And that is a tremendously radical standpoint. Not that *you* will be liberated, but liberated *from you.*

The only freedom that Buddha says is real freedom is freedom from you. Otherwise your mind will go on playing games. It will go on painting new desires on new canvases. Nothing will change. Canvases you can change. You can get out of the marketplace and sit in a temple—nothing will change, your mind will project the same desires in heaven and paradise.

Look at this mind. Look at its desires. Watch, become aware. Again and again I will have to remind you, because I am talking in non-Buddhist language. So when Buddha says become aware, he means *be awareness.* There is nobody who becomes aware; there is only awareness.

Yes, you will never be born again, but if you carry the idea that you are, then you will remain in a continuum. If you drop the idea of the self, the continuum disappears; you evaporate.

That's what nirvana is. Just as if you put off a lamp and the light ceases, disappears, you put off your desiring mind and all misery, and all transmigration, and all suffering, ceases. Suddenly, you are not there.

But that does not mean that nothing is; otherwise there will be no difference between an atheist and a Buddha. There is tremendous difference. Buddha says you cease, and for the first time reality takes over. But he never gives it any name, because naming is not possible—to name it is to falsify it. To say it is, is to be untrue to it. He keeps quiet, absolutely silent about it. He indicates the way to experience it. He does not spin and weave a philosophy around it.

Is there anything a seeker has to ask for,
or does everything happen on its own?

Everything happens on its own, but a seeker has to be alert not to miss the train.

The train comes on its own, but you have to be alert. All around you so much is happening; in twenty-four hours, awake or asleep, you have to be watchful of what is happening. And the more you are alert, you will be surprised—the same things are happening that were happening before, but the meaning has changed; the significance is different.

The rose flower is the same rose, but now it is radiant, surrounded by some new energy that you were not aware of before, a new beauty. It seems that you used to see only the outer side of the rose; now you are able to see its inner world. You used to look at the palace from the outside; now you have entered its innermost chambers. You have seen the moon hundreds of times, but when you see it silently, peacefully, meditatively, you become aware of a beauty that you were not aware of before, a beauty that is not ordinarily available, a beauty for which you need to grow some insight. And in silence, in peace, that insight grows.

It happened—a very significant incident. One of the Indian poets, Rabindranath Tagore, translated one of his small books of poems, *Gitanjali (Offering of Songs)*. He was awarded the Nobel Prize for that small book. In India, it was available for at least fifteen years. But unless a book meets the international standards of language and gains international appreciation, it is difficult for it to get a Nobel Prize. Rabindranath himself was a little worried, because he translated it—and to translate poetry is always a very difficult affair. To translate prose is simple; to translate poetry is immensely difficult, because prose is of the marketplace and poetry is something of the world of love, of the world of beauty, of the world of moon and stars.

It is a delicate affair. And every language has its own nuances that are almost untranslatable. So although the poet himself translated his own poetry, he was doubtful about the translation. He showed it to one of the Christian missionaries, a very famous man of those days, C. F. Andrews—a very literate, cultured, sophisticated man.

Andrews suggested four changes. He said, "Everything else is right, but in four places it is not grammatically correct." So Rabindranath simply accepted his advice and changed those four places.

His friend, the Irish poet Yeats, called together a meeting in London of English poets, to hear Rabindranath's translation. Everybody appreciated it; the beauty of it was something absolutely new to the Western world. But Yeats, who was the most prominent poet of England in those days, said, "Everything else is right, but in four places, it seems that somebody who is not a poet has made some changes."

Rabindranath could not believe it. He said, "Where are those four places?"

Yeats pointed out the four places that Rabindranath had changed, following the advice of C. F. Andrews. Rabindranath said, "What is wrong with those lines?"

Yeats said, "There is nothing wrong, they are grammatically correct. But poetically . . . whoever suggested them is a man who knows his grammar but does not know poetry. He is a man of the mind but not a man of the heart. The flow is obstructed, as if a river had come across a rock."

Rabindranath told him, "I had asked C. F. Andrews to look at it; these are his words. I will tell you the words that I had in these places before." And when he put his words in, Yeats said, "They are perfectly right, although grammatically wrong. But grammar is not important. When it is a question of poetry, grammar is not important. You change it back, and use your own words."

I have always thought that there are ways of the mind and there are ways of the heart; they need not be supportive of each other. And if it happens that the mind is not in agreement with the heart, then the mind is wrong. Its agreement or disagreement does not matter. What matters is that your heart feels at ease, peaceful, silent, harmonious, at home.

We are trained for the mind, so our mind is very articulate. And nobody takes any notice of the heart. In fact, it is pushed aside by everybody because it is of no use in the marketplace, it is no use in the world of ambitions, no use in politics, no use in business.

But with me, the situation is just the opposite: The mind is of no use. The heart knows best.

Everything happens, just your heart has to be ready to receive it. Everything comes, but if your heart is closed . . . the secret laws of life are such that the doors of your heart will not even be knocked upon.

Existence knows how to wait; it can wait for eternity. It all depends on you. Everything is ready to happen any moment. Just open all your doors, all your windows, so that existence can pour into you from every side. There is no other god than existence, and there is no other paradise than your very being. When existence pours into your being, paradise has entered into you—or, you have entered into paradise, just different ways of saying the same thing. But remember: Nothing is expected of you.

All the religions have been telling you for centuries that you have to do this, you have to do that. That you have to be a torturer of yourself, you have to renounce pleasures, you have to fight with your body, you have to renounce the world. The Buddhist scriptures have 33,000 principles that a seeker should follow. It is almost impossible to remember them; following them is out of the question! I don't have a single principle for you to follow, just a simple understanding that it is your life—enjoy it, allow it to sing a song in you, allow it to become a dance in you. You have nothing else to do but simply to be available, and flowers are going to shower on you.

4

Destiny, Fate, and Karma

Existence gives you birth as tabula rasa. No fate is written; there is no destiny such that whatever you do, it has to happen.

Existence is freedom. Fate is slavery. Freedom means it is up to you to decide what is going to happen. Fate is a bogus hypothesis.

Trust is a totally different thing. Trust is not fate. Trust simply means that "Whatever happens, I am part of existence, and existence cannot be intentionally inimical to me. If sometimes I feel that it is, it must be my misunderstanding."

Are our lives predestined or not?

This is not a personal problem; it is a philosophical question.

Our lives are both predestined and they are not. Both yes and no. And both answers are true for all questions about life.

In a way, everything is predetermined. Whatever is physical in you, material, whatever is mental, is predetermined. But something in you constantly remains undetermined, unpredictable. That something is your consciousness.

If you are identified with your body and your material existence, in the same proportion you are determined by cause and effect. Then you are a machine. But if you are not identified with your material existence, with either body or mind—if you can feel yourself as something separate, different, above and transcendent to body–mind—then that transcending consciousness is not predetermined. It is spontaneous, free. Consciousness means freedom; matter means slavery. So it depends on how you define yourself. If you say, "I am only the body," then everything about you is completely determined.

A person who says that man is only the body cannot say that man is not predetermined. Ordinarily, those who do not believe in such a thing as consciousness don't believe in predetermination, either. People who are religious and believe in consciousness are ordinarily those who believe in predetermination. So what I am saying may look very contradictory, but still, it is the case.

A person who has known consciousness has known freedom. So only a spiritual person can say there is no determination at all. That realization comes only when you are completely unidentified with the body. If you feel that you are just a material existence, then no freedom is possible. With matter, no freedom is possible. Matter means that which cannot be free; it must flow in the chain of cause and effect.

Once someone has achieved consciousness, enlightenment, he is completely out of the realm of cause and effect. He becomes absolutely unpredictable, you cannot say anything about him. He begins to live each moment; his existence becomes atomic.

Your existence is a riverlike chain in which every step is determined by the past. Your future is not really future; it is just a by-product of the past. It is only the past determining, shaping, formulating, and conditioning your future. That is why your future is predictable.

B. F. Skinner says that man is as predictable as anything else; the only difficulty is that we have not yet devised the means to know his total past. The moment we can know his past, we can predict everything about him. Based upon the people he has worked with, Skinner is right, because they are all ultimately predictable. He has experimented with hundreds of people, and he has found that they are all mechanical beings, that nothing exists within them that can be called freedom.

But his study is limited; no buddha has gone to his laboratory to be experimented upon. If even one person is free, if even one person is not mechanical, not predictable, Skinner's whole theory falls apart. If one person in the whole history of mankind is free and unpredictable, then all human beings are potentially free and unpredictable.

The whole possibility of freedom depends on whether you emphasize your body or your consciousness. If your whole flow of life is just outward, then everything is determined. Or are you something inner also? Do not give any preformulated answer. Do not say, "I am the soul." If you feel there is nothing inside you, then be honest about it. This honesty will be the first step toward the inner freedom of consciousness.

If you go deeply inside, you will feel that everything is just part of the outside. Your body has come from without, your thoughts have come from without, even your "self" has been given to you by others. That is why you are so fearful of the opinion of others, because they are completely in control of your self. They can change their opinion of you at any moment. Your self, your body, your thoughts are given to you by others, so what is inside? You are layers and layers of outside accumulation. If you are identified with this personality of yours that comes from others, then everything is determined.

Become aware of everything that comes from the outside and become nonidentified with it. Then a moment will come when the outside falls away completely. You will be in a vacuum. This vacuum is the passage between the outside and the inside, the door. We are so afraid of the vacuum, so afraid of being empty that we cling to the outside accumulations. One has to be courageous enough to disidentify with the accumulation and to remain in the vacuum. If you are not courageous enough, you will go out and cling to something, and be filled with it. But this moment of being in the vacuum is meditation. If you are courageous enough, if you can remain in this moment, soon your whole being will automatically turn inward.

When there is nothing to be attached to from the outside, your being turns inward. Then you know for the first time that you are something that transcends everything you have been thinking yourself to be. Now you are something different from becoming; you are *being*. This being is free; nothing can determine it. It is absolute freedom. No chain of cause and effect is possible.

Your actions are related to past actions. A created a situation for B to become possible; B creates a situation in which C flowers. Your acts are connected to past acts and this goes back to the beginningless beginning, and on to the endless end. Not only do your own acts determine you, but your father's and mother's acts also have a continuity with yours. Your society, your history, all that has happened before, is somehow related to your present act. The whole history has come to flower in you. Everything that has ever happened is connected with your act, so your act is obviously determined. It is such a minute part of the whole picture. History is such a vital, living force and your individual act is such a small part of it.

Marx said that it is not consciousness that determines the conditions of society. It is society and its conditions that determine consciousness. It is not that great men create great societies; it is great societies that create great men. And he is right in a way, because you are not the originator of your actions. The whole of history has determined them; you are just carrying them out.

The whole evolutionary process has gone into the making of your biological cells. These cells in you can then become part of another person. You may think that you are the father of a child, but you have just been a stage on which the whole biological evolution has acted and has forced you to act. The act of procreation is so forceful because it is beyond you; it is the whole evolutionary process working through you.

This is one way in which acts happen in relation to other, past acts. But when a person becomes enlightened, a new phenomenon begins to happen. Acts are no longer connected with past acts. Any act, now, is connected only with his consciousness. It comes from his consciousness, not from the past. That is why an enlightened person cannot be predicted.

Skinner says that we can determine what you will do if your past acts are known. He says that the old proverb, "You can lead a horse to water, but you can't make him drink," is wrong. You can force him to. You can create an atmosphere so that the horse will have to drink. The horse can be forced, and you also can be forced because your actions are created by situations, by circumstances. But even though you can bring a buddha to the river, you cannot force him to drink. The more you try to force him, the more impossible it will be. No heat will make him do it; even if a thousand suns shine on him, it will not help. A buddha has a different origin of action. It is not concerned with other acts; it is connected with consciousness.

That is why I emphasize that you act consciously. Then, every moment you act. It is not a question of a continuation of other acts. You are free. Now you begin to act, and no one can say how you will act.

Habits are mechanical; they repeat themselves. The more you repeat something, the more efficient you become. Efficiency means that now consciousness is no longer needed. If a person is an efficient typist, it means that no effort is needed; typing can be done unconsciously. Even if he is thinking about something else, the typing continues. The body is typing; the person is not needed. Efficiency means that the thing is so certain that no effort is possible. With freedom, effort is always possible. A machine cannot make errors. To err, one has to be conscious.

So your acts have a chain relationship with your previous acts; they are determined. Your childhood determines your youth; your youth determines your old age; your birth determines your death; everything is determined. Buddha used to say, "Provide the cause, and the effect will be there." This is the world of cause and effect in which everything is determined.

If you act with total consciousness, an altogether different situation exists. Then everything is moment to moment. Consciousness is a flow; it is not static. It is life itself, so it changes. It is alive. It goes on expanding; it goes on becoming new, fresh, young. Then, your acts will be spontaneous.

I am reminded of a Zen story. . . .

A Zen master asked his disciple a particular question. The question was answered exactly as it should be answered. The next day the master asked exactly the same question. The disciple said, "But I answered this question yesterday."

The master said, "Now I am asking you again." The disciple repeated the same answer. The master said, "You do not know!"

The disciple said, "But yesterday I answered in the same way and you nodded your head. So I interpreted that the answer was right. Why have you changed your mind now?"

The master said, "Anything that can be repeated is not coming from you. The answer has come from your memory, not from your consciousness. If you had really known, the answer would be different because so much has changed. I am not the same man who asked you this question yesterday. The whole situation is different; you also are different—but the answer is the same. I had to ask the question again just to see if you would repeat the answer. Nothing can be repeated."

The more alive you are, the less repetitive. Only a dead man can be consistent. Living is inconsistency; life is freedom. Freedom cannot be consistent. Consistent with what? You can be consistent only with the past.

An enlightened person is consistent only in his consciousness; he is never consistent with his past. He is totally in the act. Nothing is left behind; nothing is left out. The next moment the act is finished and his consciousness is fresh again. Consciousness will be there whenever any situation arises, but each act will be made in complete freedom, as if it is the first time that this man has been in this particular situation.

That is why I answered both yes and no to your question. It depends on you, whether you are consciousness, or whether you are an accumulation, a bodily existence.

Religiousness gives freedom because religiousness gives consciousness. The more science knows about matter, the more the world will be enslaved. The whole phenomenon of matter is of cause and effect: if you know that given *this, that* happens, then everything can be determined.

In the coming decades, we will see the whole course of humanity being determined in many ways. The greatest calamity that is possible is not nuclear warfare. It can only destroy. The real calamity will come from the psychological sciences. They will learn how a human being can be completely controlled. Because we are not conscious, we can be made to behave in predetermined ways.

As we are, everything about us is determined. Someone is Hindu; someone else is Mohammedan—this is predetermination, not freedom. Parents have decided; society is deciding. Someone is a doctor and someone else is an engineer; now his behavior is determined. We are already being controlled constantly, and our methods are still very primitive. Newer techniques will be able to determine our behavior to such an extent that no one will be able to say that there is a soul. If your every response is determined, then what is the meaning of the soul?

Your responses can be determined through body chemistry. If alcohol is given to you, you behave differently. Your body chemistry is different, so you behave differently. At one time, the ultimate tantra technique was to take intoxicants and remain conscious. If a person remained conscious when everything indicated that he should be unconscious, only then would tantra say he was enlightened—otherwise not. If body chemistry can change your consciousness, then what is the meaning of consciousness? If an injection can make you unconscious, then what is the meaning? Then the chemical drug in the injection is more powerful than your own consciousness. Tantra says it is possible to transcend every intoxicant and remain conscious. The stimulus has been given, but the response is not there.

Sex is a chemical phenomenon; a particular quantity of a particular hormone creates sexual desire. You *become* the desire. You may repent when your body chemistry has returned to its normal level, but the repentance is meaningless. When the hormones are there again, you will act in the same way. So tantra has also experimented with sex. If you feel no sexual desire in a situation that is totally sexual, then you are free. Your body chemistry has been left far behind. The body is there, but you are not in the body.

Anger is also just chemistry. Biochemists will soon be able to make you anger-proof, or sex-proof, but you will not be a buddha. Buddha was not incapable of anger. He was capable of it, but the effect of feeling anger was not there.

If your body chemistry is controlled, you will be incapable of being angry. The chemical condition that makes you feel angry is not there, so the effect of anger is not there. Or if your sex hormones are eliminated from your body, you will not be sexual. But the real thing is not whether you are sexual or not, or angry or not. The real thing is how to be aware in a situation that requires your unawareness, how to be conscious in a situation that happens only in unconsciousness.

Whenever such a situation is there, meditate on it. You have been given a great opportunity. If you feel jealous, meditate on it. This is the right moment. Your body chemistry is working within you. It will make you unconscious; it will make you behave as if you are mad. Now, be conscious. Let there be jealousy, do not suppress it, but be conscious; be a witness to it.

If there is anger, be a witness to it; if there is sex, be a witness to it. Let whatever is happening inside you happen, and begin to meditate on the whole situation. By and by, the more your awareness deepens, the less possibility there is of your behavior being determined for you. You become free. *Moksha*, freedom, doesn't mean anything else. It only means a consciousness that is so free that now nothing can determine it.

Is the degree of spiritual progress predestined? Or is one's life a series of challenges and possibilities without anything being known about the outcome?

The essence is predestined; the personality is just an accident. That which you are is predestined, that which you appear to be is just an accident. Your being a Hindu, your being a Christian is an accident. Your being a man, your being a woman is an accident.

Your being a German or an Indian is an accident. Your being black or white is an accident. But your *being,* simply your being, is destined.

Try to find that which is destined, and don't be too concerned with that which is irrelevant, accidental.

Your nose is a little long or a little short. Don't be bothered much about it; it is just accidental. Or your skin has a pigment and you are black. Or your skin doesn't have that pigment—not worth more than four pennies. Don't be too worried about it. It is just irrelevant.

Try to find that which is absolutely destined. That is your nature; that is your essence.

But you are lost in accidents. You pay too much attention to accidents; you are too worried about them. Your whole time and energy are wasted in them. You become so occupied with the non-essential that the essential is forgotten.

This is the state of the man who is asleep: always focused on the nonessential. Thinking of money, thinking of power, thinking of the house, thinking of the car, thinking of this and that—but never looking at that which is your innermost core, which is you. That innermost core is absolutely destined. Outside, nothing is destined. Inside, everything is destined. Pay more attention to it. That's what *sannyas* is all about: a turning toward the essential, and a turning away from the nonessential.

I am not saying that you don't eat, that you don't live in a house—no. That is not the meaning. Live in a house, but don't be too concerned. One has to eat to live. Eat—but don't make eating your whole business. There are people who continuously think of eating.

Money is needed, but don't make money your god. Use it when you have it. When you don't have it, then use that non-having also, because that has its own beauties. When you have money, you can have a palace. Have it. When you don't have the money, become a vagabond and live under the sky. That has its own beauty. When you have money, use it. Don't be used by the money. When you don't have it, enjoy poverty. Richness has its own richness, poverty has its own richness also. There are many things that only a poor man can enjoy—never a rich man. There are many things only rich people can enjoy—never a poor man. So, whatsoever opportunity . . . When you are rich, enjoy that which a rich man can enjoy. Whenever you are poor, enjoy that which poor men enjoy.

But what do you do?—you do just the reverse. When you are rich, you long for those things that only poor men can enjoy. And when you are poor, you long for those things that only a rich man can enjoy. You are simply foolish; I don't see any intelligence in it.

I was staying with a friend. He was a vice-chancellor, an old man, a drunkard—almost always drunk—but he was a very good man, as drunkards are always. A very sweet, a very polite, a very loving man.

In the night, he had taken too much drink, and I was sitting with him. He became suddenly afraid. He became so paranoid that he told me: "Please write a letter immediately to the police station—tell them to send two intelligence officers."

I wrote the letter, but I committed an error. I wrote to the police superintendent: "Please send two *intelligent* officers."

The old drunkard looked at the letter and started laughing and said: "Who has ever heard of intelligent officers? Write 'intelligence officers,' not 'intelligent officers.'"

It is almost impossible to find an intelligent officer, because it is almost impossible to find an intelligent man. Intelligence is absolutely lacking.

When you have money, enjoy it. Live like a king when you have it. But I see people—they have money and they live like beggars. They are saving it for the future, and when it is lost, then they start thinking about it: "Why did we waste the opportunity? We should have enjoyed."

Poor persons, poor people, always thinking about living in palaces while they can enjoy the tree where they are. The singing birds, and the sun, and the air—the world is more open to a poor man. A poor man can enjoy a beautiful sleep, because for a rich man, sleep has become difficult. He may have better bedrooms, he may have more comfortable mattresses, but he will not be able to sleep. Then he will think about beggars and will feel envious and jealous that these poor people are sleeping so well, snoring, and "I cannot sleep."

When you can sleep well, sleep well. When you have beautiful mattresses, enjoy them—and suffer insomnia! But be intelligent.

Why is it that sincere, gentle, and kindhearted people suffer and are neglected? Why is it that cunning, greedy, and evil people are flourishing and respectable? Is it the result of their past life karma, their fate?

There is no need to believe in fate. There is no need to believe that people are suffering because of their past evil acts, karma. The reality is that the good people, the nice people, the virtuous people are bound to suffer. You cannot have everything in life. If you have goodness, enjoy it; if you have virtue, enjoy it; if you have niceness, enjoy it.

Why should you be jealous of the cunning people becoming prime ministers, of the evil people becoming rich? The evil people are bound to win in the race with the good people if the race is for money, if the race is for power, prestige, respectability. But if the race is for inner silence, peace, calm, coolness, silence, meditation, godliness, then the evil people will not get anything, anywhere. I don't see any problem at all. If you had asked this to anybody else, he would have explained it through past lives because there seems to be no other way for the logicians, for the theologians.

They have been telling you that good people should not suffer, that evil people should suffer. But in life, you see just the opposite happening: good people are suffering; evil people are on the top, enjoying. Naturally, the theologian has to create a fiction of past life, of faith, of *prarabdha*, of karma—all bogus and fictitious things. The reality is very simple: Goodness has nothing to do with earning money. Goodness earns something more valuable; it earns peace of mind.

The virtuous person need not be worried about mundane things. He may not have a palace, but he will live more blissfully in his hut than a king lives in his palace. The virtuous will not be able to manage a palace, but he will be able to manage blissfulness. The cunning will manage to reach to the palace, but he will lose all peace of mind, he will lose all contact with himself.

So it is very simple to me. If you want the inner world and inner riches, be good, be virtuous, be nice, and don't be jealous of those poor people who are simply cunning and earning money, who are doing every kind of criminal act and reaching to high posts and respectability. Do you want to have both? Do you want money and also meditation? You are asking too much. Something has to be left for the cunning, too! He is making a lot of effort. And he is suffering so much inside. You may be suffering on the outside, he is suffering inside—and that is a bigger suffering than you know of.

So I don't see that life needs to be explained by fictions. Life is simple mathematics. You get what you deserve. Just don't ask anything that is not related to your qualities, and then there is no problem. Then you will not see it the way you are seeing it—that the virtuous are suffering. No—no virtuous person is suffering. Every virtuous person is enjoying every moment blissfully. And if he is suffering, then he is not virtuous: he is simply a coward. Basically he is cunning, but he is not courageous. He wants the same things that the cunning man has, but he is not courageous enough to be cunning, nor is he clever enough to be cunning. Cunningness is an art.

The cunning should have what they can manage. The evil ones should have what they can manage. But the good ones don't have to be jealous, because they have the real treasures of the innermost being. They should be compassionate. They should see those poor, cunning politicians, the super-rich—they should see their inner poverty, their inner darkness, their inner hell, and they should be compassionate, not competitive!

Can it not be argued that karma, with its natural forces of cause and effect, should not be interfered with? Or is it also the way of existence to bring such a possibility within the reach of the evolving world, the evolving soul?

Everything can be argued, but argument leads nowhere. You can argue, but how is that argument going to help you? You can argue that the natural process of karma should not be interfered with—don't interfere then. But then be happy in your misery—and you are not. You want to interfere. If you can rely on the natural process, it is just wonderful—but then don't make any complaint. Don't ask, "Why is this so?" It is so because of the natural process of karma. You are suffering?—you are suffering because of the natural process of karma, and otherwise is not possible; don't interfere.

This is what the doctrine of fate, of kismet is—the doctrine of believing in fate. Then you are not to do anything: whatsoever is happening is happening, and you have to accept it. Then, too, it becomes a surrender, and you need not do anything. But then total acceptance is needed. Really there is no need to interfere, but can you be in such a state where you don't interfere? You are constantly interfering with everything. You cannot leave it to nature. If you can leave it, then nothing else is needed and everything will happen to you. But if you cannot leave it, then interfere. And you can interfere, but the process has to be understood.

Really, meditating is not interfering in the process of karma; rather, it is taking a jump out of it. Exactly it is not interfering; it is taking a jump out of the vicious wheel, out of the vicious circle. The circle will go on, and the process will come to an end by itself. You cannot put an end to it, but you can be out of it, and once you are out of it, it becomes illusory.

For example, Ramana Maharashi died of cancer. His disciples tried to persuade him to go for treatment. He said, "Okay. If you like it and if it will make you happy, then treat me. But as far as I am concerned, it is okay." The doctors were surprised, because his

139

body was suffering, it was in deep pain, but his eyes were without any pain. His body was suffering deeply, but he was not suffering.

The body is part of the karma, it is part of the mechanical circle of cause and effect, but the consciousness can be beyond it, it can transcend it. He was just a witness. He was seeing that the body was suffering, that the body was going to die, but he was a witness. He was not interfering with it, not interfering at all. He was just watching whatsoever was happening, but he was not in the vicious circle, he was not identified, he was not within it then.

Meditation is not an interference. Really, without meditation, you are interfering every moment. With meditation you go be-yond; you become a watcher on the hill. Deep down in the valley things go on, they continue, but they don't belong to you. You are just an onlooker. It is as if they are happening to somebody else, or as if they are happening in a dream, or in a film on the screen. You are not interfering. You are just not within the drama itself—you have come out. Now you are not an actor: you have become a spec-tator. This is the only change.

And when you are just a witness, the body will complete im-mediately whatsoever has to be completed. If you have many kar-mas for suffering, and now that you have become a witness you are not going to be reborn again, the body will have to suffer in this life all the suffering that would have been in many lives. So it hap-pens many times that an enlightened man has to suffer many bodily ills, because now there is no future birth, no future life. This is going to be the last body, so all the karmas and the whole process has to be completed, finished.

So it happens that if we look at Jesus' life through Eastern eyes, then the crucifixion is a different phenomenon. To the Western mind, there is no succession of lives, no rebirth, no reincarnation, so they don't really have a very deep analysis of the crucifixion. They have a myth that Jesus suffered for us, his suffering was a salvation for us. But this is absurd; and this is not true to the facts also, because if Jesus' suffering has become a salvation for you, then why is humanity still suffering? It is suffering more than it ever suffered before.

After Jesus' crucifixion, humanity has not entered into the Kingdom of God. If he suffered for us, if his crucifixion was a repentance of our guilt and sin, then he is a failure, because the guilt continues, the sin continues, the suffering continues. Then his suffering was in vain, then the crucifixion didn't succeed.

Christianity has simply a myth. But the Eastern analysis of human life has a different attitude. Jesus' crucifixion was all his suffering accumulated through his own karmas. And this was his last life, he would not enter the body again, so the whole suffering had to be crystallized, concentrated, in a single point. That single point became the crucifixion.

He did not suffer for anyone else—no one can suffer for anyone else. He suffered for himself, for his past karmas. No one can make you free; you are in bondage because of your karmas, so how can Jesus make you free? He can make himself a slave, he can make himself a free man, he can liberate himself. Through the crucifixion, the account of his own karmas closed. He was finished, the chain had come to an end. Cause and effect—they had come to an end. This body would not be born again; he would not enter into another womb. If he was not an enlightened person, then he would have had to suffer all this for many lives. It became concentrated in one point, in one life.

You cannot interfere, and if you interfere, you will create more misery for yourself. Don't interfere with karmas, but go beyond, be a witness to them. Take them as a dream, not real; just look at them and be indifferent. Don't get involved. Your body suffers— look at the suffering. Your body is happy—look at the happiness. Don't get identified—that's all that meditation means.

And don't find alibis, don't find excuses. Don't say that "this can be argued." You can argue anything, you are free to, but remember that your argument may be suicidal. You can argue against yourself, and you can create an argument that is not going to help you, that is not going to transform you, rather, that is going to become a hindrance. We go on arguing.

Just today one girl came to meet me. She asked me, "Tell me, is there really a God?" She was ready to argue that there is no God. I looked at her face, her eyes. She was tense, filled with argument; she wanted to fight about the point. Really deep down she wanted me to say that there is no God, because if there is God, you are in trouble. If there is God, then you cannot remain whatsoever you are; then a challenge comes. God is a challenge. It means you cannot be satisfied with yourself; something higher than you is possible. A higher state, an absolute state of consciousness is possible. That's what God means.

So she was ready to argue, and she said, "I am an atheist and I don't believe in God."

I told her, "If there is no God, how can you 'not believe in' him? And God is irrelevant. Your belief and your disbelief, your argument for and your argument against are related to you; they are not related to God. Why are you concerned? If there is no God, why have you traveled so long, and why have you come to me to argue about something that is not? Forget and forgive him. Go home, don't waste your time. If he is not, then why are you worried? Why this effort to prove that he is not? This effort shows something about you. You are afraid. If God is, then it is a challenge. If God is not, then you can remain whatsoever you are; there is no challenge to life."

A person who is afraid of challenges, risks, dangers, of changing himself, of mutation, will always deny that there is God. The denial is his mind; the denial shows something about him, not about God.

I told her that God is not a thing that can be proved or disproved. God is not an object about which we can take some opinion for or against. Godliness is a possibility within you. It is not something without; it is a possibility within you. If you travel to that possibility, it becomes real. If you don't travel up to that point, it is unreal. And if you argue against it, then there is no point in traveling; you remain the same. And this becomes a vicious circle.

You argue that God is not, and because of it you never travel toward godliness—because it is an inner travel, an inner journey. You never travel, because how can you travel toward a point that is not? So you remain the same. And when you remain the same, you never meet, you never encounter the divine. You never come to any feeling, to any vibration from something beyond. Then it is proved more for you that it does not exist. And the more it is proved, the more you are far away, the more you are falling, the more the gap increases.

So it is not a question of whether God exists or not, I told her. It is a question of whether you want to grow or not. If you grow, your total growth will be the meeting, your total growth will be the communion, your total growth will be the encounter. I told her one anecdote.

One windy morning, just as the spring was ending, a snail started traveling upward on a cherry tree. Some sparrows that were just on a neighboring oak started laughing, because it was not the season and there were no cherries on the tree, and this poor snail was making so much effort to reach the top. They laughed at his expense.

Then one sparrow flew down, came near to the snail and said, "Darling, where are you going? There are no cherries yet on the tree."

But the snail never even paused; she continued her upward journey. Without pausing, the snail said, "But they will be there when I reach. They will be there when I reach there. It will take a long time for me to reach to the top, and by that time cherries will be there."

God is not, but godliness will be there by the time you reach. It is not something that is already there—it is never there. It is a growth. It is your own growth. When you reach to a point where you are totally conscious, godliness is. But don't argue. Rather than wasting your energy in arguing, use your energy in transforming yourself.

And energy is not much. If you divert your energy into argument, you can become a genius in arguing. But then you are wasting your energy, and it is at a great cost, because the same energy can become meditation. You can become a logician: you can make very logical arguments, you can find very convincing proofs or disproofs, but you will remain the same. Your arguments are not going to change you.

Remember one thing: Whatsoever changes you is good. Whatsoever gives you growth, expansion, increase in consciousness, is good. Whatsoever makes you static and whatsoever protects your status quo is not good; it is fatal, suicidal.

> *There is a Sufi saying that "No human being can avoid his fate. This is a world of limitations—blessed are those who gain a taste of the limitless, despite this fact."*
>
> *A famous astrologer and composer, Dane Rudhyar, who was a friend of George Gurdjieff, said, "The old idea of astrology—that experience happens to human beings—is not true. On the contrary, human beings happen to their experience."*
>
> *My observation is that every astrologer who is courageous enough will find out that Gurdjieff is right when he says, "Man is a machine."*

George Gurdjieff is right when he says that man is a machine, but by *man* he means all those who are living unconsciously, who are not aware, who are not awake, who do not respond to reality but only react. Ninety-nine point nine percent of human beings come in the category of machines. With these machines, astrology is possible.

In fact, predictions can be made, guarantees can be issued only about machines. A watch can be guaranteed for five years, a car can be guaranteed for a certain time because we know the capacity of the machine, how much it can work, how long it can go. Its scope is limited. And it cannot do anything on its own, it can only react to situations—which are almost predictable.

For example, at a certain stage a boy and a girl will become sexually mature, and their hormones and their biology will start forcing them toward each other. They will call it love because nobody wants to be categorized as a machine. But two machines cannot love, two machines can only be together, can struggle, can stumble against each other.

And it is not coincidence that in every language, love is called "falling in love." It is an unconscious process; it is a fall. You cannot answer why you love a certain person.

And now the science of human biology, genetics, has grown much more mature. It is possible to inject hormones into you that can make all your love disappear, or that can make you a great lover. But these are hormones; it is chemical. You are not consciously involved in it.

It happened in Mumbai near about twenty years ago—an astrologer came to see me. I told him, "You will be disappointed. Astrology won't work with me."

He said, "It is not a question of you or anybody else: there are no exceptions in astrology."

I said, "Then do one thing: Write down twelve things that I am going to do in one year. You keep one copy and I will keep one copy, and I will write on both copies that these are the twelve things that I will *not* do. That's the only way to decide whether your astrology works or not."

He got a little afraid because he had not thought of this possibility. I said, "Even to the extent that if you say that I will live, I will die—just to make the point clear that astrology won't work with me."

He said, "Now I have to study more in depth. And after three days I will come back."

Twenty years have passed; he has not come back! Whenever I have gone to Mumbai, I have inquired, "Phone the astrologer and ask when that in-depth study is going to be complete—because twenty years have passed. Has he dropped the idea?"

If you are enlightened, then astrology cannot function for you. Then you can love, then you can do, then you can act, then you have a certain mastery over your own being. But unconscious, you are just moving hither and thither as the wind blows. And anybody who has studied human nature deeply . . .

There are many astrological schools that have studied for centuries how the mechanical man works. They have come to certain conclusions, and their conclusions are almost always correct. If they are incorrect, that means the astrologer is not well prepared, his studies in human nature and unconscious behavior are not complete.

But the moment you start becoming conscious, you start becoming really a human being—not a machine.

When Gurdjieff said for the first time that man is a machine, it shocked many people. But he was saying the truth. It is just that the truth is applicable only to 99.9 percent of people—0.1 percent of people have to be left out of it.

Gautam Buddha was born. . . . And in the East those were the days of the highest possibilities for human genius. In all the directions in which the East was working, it reached the very peak, the climax . . . to such an extent that you cannot find a new yoga posture; Patañjali exhausted all the possibilities of postures, the science is complete. Five thousand years have passed, and in five thousand years thousands of people have tried, but there is no way to find a new posture. You cannot find a new sex posture; Vatsyayana completed all the postures possible—and a few that may even look impossible! Shiva completed all the meditation techniques—112. You can play with new combinations, but nothing new is possible.

Astrology was at its peak. And as Gautam Buddha was born, the son of a great king, the king immediately called the best astrologers. They all studied the birth chart and they all remained silent.

Only one—a young astrologer—said to the king, "These people are silent because this is a strange boy, and we cannot be decisive about him. There are two possibilities"—and astrology never speaks in that way. Astrology means you have to predict what is going to happen; you are not there to predict all the possibilities. That will not be prediction.

But the young astrologer said, "These are old wise people, so they will not even say this. I am young and I can stick my neck out, I can risk, because I don't have any reputation. There are two possibilities: either this boy will become an emperor of the world, a world conqueror, or he will become an enlightened, awakened liberated soul—but then he will be a beggar. Either he will be the emperor of the whole world or he will be just a beggar with a begging bowl in his hands. And it is not in our power to say what the outcome will be."

And all the old astrologers agreed. "The young man is right. We were silent because this is not the way astrology functions—we have to say, 'This is definitely going to happen.' But about this boy, we cannot say. And the possibilities are so diametrically opposite—either the emperor or the beggar."

And that's what happened.

The king asked all those wise astrologers, "Then tell me how to protect him so that he does not move toward becoming a beggar but becomes the world emperor. That has been my lifelong desire. I could not achieve it, but he has the possibility! So just tell me how to prevent him from becoming a beggar."

They gave all their advice, and their advice turned out to create just the opposite of what they intended. They had suggested, "Give him all the luxuries. Don't let him know about death, old age. Don't let him know about becoming a seeker, a *sannyasin*. He should not be given time to think, 'What is the meaning of life?' Keep him engaged continually in singing, in dancing, wine and women, drown him completely."

And that's what created the trouble—because for twenty-nine years he was kept so isolated from the world, so ignorant about the ordinary reality of the world where people become sick, people become old, people die, where there are *sannyasins*, there are seekers of truth . . . If he had been allowed from the very beginning, he would have become immune—from the very beginning he would have seen that people become old, people become sick, a few people become *sannyasins*. But for twenty-nine years he was kept completely aloof.

And after twenty-nine years when he came into contact with the world—one day, one has to come into contact with the world—then it was a great shock. He could not believe his eyes! He could not believe that people become old; he could not believe that life is going to end in death. He could not believe that he had been kept in darkness while there were people searching to find the meaning of life, trying to find out whether there was something immortal in man or not.

The shock would not have been so great. It is not such a shock for anybody else—from the very childhood, everything is seen and one becomes, slowly, accustomed. But for him, the shock was tremendous. That very night he left the palace as a *sannyasin* in search of truth. The father was trying to save him from the begging bowl, and that's what he adopted that night.

It was possible he might have become Alexander the Great if he had not been kept in darkness. But in a way it was good, because Alexander the Great and his kind have not helped human consciousness. This man alone, with his begging bowl, raised humanity more than anybody else toward the stars, toward immortality, toward truth.

About such a man, astrology is not possible.

It is good to accept that you are functioning like a machine. Don't feel offended—because if you feel offended, you will defend yourself and you will remain what you are.

Try to understand your behavior—is it mechanical or not? Somebody insults you—how do you react? Is that reaction mechanical or conscious? Do you think before you become angry? Do you meditate for a moment before you respond? Perhaps what the man has said is right, and if you had not become angry immediately, instantly, without giving a small gap for meditation, you might have been grateful to the man rather than being angry. You might have said, "You are right."

In fact, things that are right hurt you much more. Lies don't hurt you at all.

Just the other day, I saw a newspaper clipping. A Western traveler coming from Tibet gave his first press conference, and in the press conference he said, "My greatest experience was meeting

with Osho in Tibet." Now people can lie like anything, and whoever reads it will believe it. The printed word has a certain impact
on people. Just a few days before, there was another news item—no
ifs and no buts, a certainty – saying that "Osho is going to appear
in Israel very soon. He has decided to become converted to Judaism, and after converting to Judaism, he will declare himself to be
the reincarnation of Moses."

Now what can you do with these people? You can laugh, but
you cannot be angry. You can enjoy, you can thank them for their
imagination. These are the people who keep the world going!

Just watch your actions and try not to be mechanical. Try
to do something that you have never done before in the same
situation.

That's what the meaning is when Jesus says, "When somebody
slaps your face, give him the other cheek, too." The real meaning
is, simply act nonmechanically—because the mechanical thing
would be when somebody slaps you, you slap him. Or if you are
not capable of slapping him right now, then wait for the right moment. But to give him the other cheek is behaving nonmechanically, is behaving very consciously.

But people can make anything mechanical.

I have heard about a Christian saint who was constantly quoting the same thing: "Love your enemy, and if somebody slaps you
on one cheek, give him the other, too."

One day a man who was against Christianity found the saint
alone, hit him hard on one of his cheeks, looked into the eyes of the
saint. . . . For a moment the saint wanted to hit him back—but being a saint, remembering all his teachings and remembering that
this man sits in his congregation in the front, he gave him the other

cheek, thinking that he would not hit it. The man hit him harder on the other cheek!—and that very moment the saint jumped on the man, hitting him hard on the nose. The man said, "What are you doing? You are a Christian, you have to love your enemy."

He said, "Forget all about it. Jesus only talked about two cheeks—about the third, I am free. Now there is no third cheek to give you. And he has not said that when he hits you on the second, give him your nose, too!" Because Jesus has not said why. . . .

Gautam Buddha in one of his sermons said, "Try to be nonmechanical as much as possible. If somebody hits you, insults you, humiliates you, forgive him seven times. Be conscious."

Jesus was saying only one time—because you have only two cheeks, and one he has hit already. Only one is left, so there is not much. . . . Buddha is saying seven times.

One of the disciples stood up and said, "What about the eighth? Seven times we will keep patience, but what about the eighth?"

Even Buddha was silent for a moment. So deep is man's mechanicalness. . . . He said, "Then change it, make it seventy-seven times."

The man said, "You can make it any number, but the question will remain the same—what about the seventy-eighth time? We can wait seventy-seven times. . . ."

You can behave in a saintly way, but if it is mechanical, it doesn't change anything.

Be alert and see that yesterday you have done the same thing. Today make a little difference—you are not a machine. You said the same thing to your wife, make a little difference—you are not a machine. And if in twenty-four hours' time you continually go on changing, slowly you will slip out of the mechanical behavior and a consciousness will arise in you.

That consciousness makes you really human. Before, you only appear human; in reality you are not.

5

In Search of Freedom

Let me remind you: Don't take life for granted. It has to be created, and it can be created only by choosing freely, by choosing on your own. Yes, there is a possibility you may go astray, there is a possibility you may commit errors, mistakes. But nothing to be worried about—mistakes and errors and going astray, they are all part of growth. It is only by committing mistakes that one learns; it is only by going astray that one comes back to the right path.

I heard you say once that the misuse of freedom is harmful. How can freedom be misused?

The philosophers have always believed that essence precedes existence, that man is born with what he is going to be already determined. Just like a seed, he contains the whole program; now the question is only of unfoldment. There is no freedom.

That has been the attitude of all the philosophers of the past: that man has a certain fate, a destiny. One is going to become a certain entity; that is fixed, the script is already written. You are not aware of it—that's another matter—but whatsoever you are doing, you are not doing it; it is being done through you by natural, unconscious forces, or by God.

This is the attitude of the determinist, the fatalist. The whole of humanity has suffered from it immensely, because this kind of approach means there is no possibility of any radical change. Nothing can be done at all about man's transformation; everything is going to happen the way it is going to happen.

It is because of this attitude that the East has suffered most. When nothing can be done, then one starts accepting everything—slavery, poverty, ugliness, one has to accept. It is not understanding, it is not awareness; it is not what Gautam the Buddha calls suchness, *tathata*. It is just despair, hopelessness hiding itself in beautiful words. But the consequence is going to be disastrous.

You can see it in India in its most developed form: the poverty, the beggars, the illness, the crippled people, the blind people. And nobody takes any note of it, because this is how life is, this is how life has always been, this is how life is always going to be. A kind of lethargy seeps into the very soul.

But the whole approach is basically false. It is a consolation, not a discovery. It is somehow to hide one's wounds—it is a rationalization. And whenever rationalizations start hiding your reality, you are bound to fall into darker and darker realms.

I would like to say to you that essence does not precede existence; on the contrary, existence precedes essence. Man is the only being on the earth who has freedom. A dog is born a dog, will live like a dog, will die like a dog; there is no freedom. A rose will remain a rose; there is no possibility of any transformation—it cannot become a lotus. There is no question of choice, there is no freedom at all. This is where man is totally different. This is the dignity of man, his specialness in existence, his uniqueness.

That's why I say Charles Darwin is not right, because he starts categorizing man with other animals; the basic difference he has not even taken note of. The basic difference is: all animals are born with a program; only man is born without a program. Man is born as a tabula rasa, a clean slate; nothing is written on it. You have to write everything that you want to write on it; it is going to be your creation.

Man is not only free—I would like to say man is freedom. That is his essential core; that's his very soul. The moment you deny freedom to man, you have denied him his most precious treasure, his very kingdom. Then he is a beggar and in a far more ugly situation than other animals, because at least they have a certain program. Then man is simply lost.

Once this is understood, that man is born *as* freedom, then all the dimensions to grow open up. Then it is up to you what to become, what not to become. It is going to be your own creation. Then life becomes an adventure—not an unfoldment but an adventure, an exploration, a discovery. The truth is not already given to you; you have to create it. In a way, each moment you are creating yourself.

If you accept the theory of fate, that is also an act of deciding about your life. By accepting fatalism, you have chosen the life of a slave—it is your choice! You have chosen to enter into a prison, you have chosen to be chained, but it is still your choice. You can come out of the prison.

That's what *sannyas* is all about: accepting your freedom. Of course people are afraid to be free, because freedom is risky. One never knows what one is doing, where one is going, what the ultimate result of it all is going to be. If you are not ready-made, then the whole responsibility is yours. You cannot throw the responsibility on somebody else's shoulders. Ultimately you will be standing before existence totally responsible for yourself, whatsoever you are, whosoever you are. You cannot shirk it; you cannot escape from it. This is the fear. Out of this fear, people have chosen all kinds of determinist attitudes.

And it is a strange thing: the religious and the irreligious are agreed only on one point, that there is no freedom. On every other point they disagree, but on one point their agreement is strange. The communists say they are atheists, irreligious, but they say that man is determined by the social, economic, political situations. Man is not free; man's consciousness is determined by outside forces. It is the same logic! You can call the outside force the economic structure; Hegel calls it History—with a capital *H*, remember—and the religious people call it God; again the word is with a capital *G*. God, history, economics, politics, society—all outside forces. But they are all agreed upon one thing: that you are not free.

This is where a really authentically religious person differs.

I say to you, you are absolutely free, unconditionally free. Don't avoid the responsibility; avoiding is not going to help. The sooner you accept it, the better, because immediately you can start creating yourself. And the moment you create yourself, great joy arises, and when you have completed yourself, the way *you* wanted it, there is immense contentment—just as when a painter finishes his painting, the last touch, and a great contentment arises in his heart. A job well done brings great peace. One feels that one has participated with existence itself.

If God is a creator, then the only prayer is to be creative, because it is only through creativity that you participate in this creativity of existence; there is no other way to participate. It has not to be thought about; you have to participate in some way. You cannot be an observer, you can only be a participant; only then will you taste the mystery of it. Creating a painting is nothing, creating a poem is nothing, creating music is nothing compared with creating yourself, creating your consciousness, creating your very being.

But people have been afraid, and there are reasons to be afraid. The first is, it is risky, because only you are responsible. Secondly, the freedom can be misused, because you can choose the wrong thing to be. Freedom means you can choose the right or the wrong; if you are only free to choose the right, it is not freedom.

Then it will be like when Ford made his first cars—they were all black. And he would take his customers into the showroom and tell them, "You can choose any color, provided it is black!"

But what kind of freedom is this? "Provided" it is right, provided it follows the Ten Commandments, provided it is according to the Gita or the Koran, provided it is according to Buddha, Mahavira, Zarathustra. Then it is not freedom at all! Freedom basically means, intrinsically means, that you are capable of both, of choosing either the right or the wrong.

And the danger is—and hence the fear—that the wrong is always easier to do. The wrong is a downhill task and the right is an uphill task. Going uphill is difficult, arduous—and the higher you go, the more arduous it becomes. But going downhill is very easy;

you need not do anything, gravitation does everything for you. You can just roll like a rock from the hilltop and the rock will reach to the very bottom; nothing has to be done. But if you want to rise in consciousness, if you want to rise in the world of beauty, truth, bliss, then you are longing for the highest peaks possible, and that certainly is difficult.

Secondly, the higher you reach, the more there is a danger of falling, because the path becomes narrow and you are surrounded on all sides by dark valleys. A single wrong step, and you will simply be gone into the abyss. You will disappear. It is more comfortable, convenient to walk on the plain ground, not to bother about the heights.

Freedom gives you the opportunity either to fall below the animals or to rise above the angels. Freedom is a ladder: one side of the ladder reaches hell; the other side touches heaven. It is the same ladder—the choice is yours, the direction has to be chosen by you.

To me, if you are not free, you cannot misuse your unfreedom; unfreedom cannot be misused. The prisoner cannot misuse his situation—he is chained, he is not free to do anything. And that is the situation of all other animals except man: they are not free. They are born to be certain kinds of animals and they will fulfill it. In fact, nature fulfills it; they are not required to do anything. There is no challenge in their life. It is only man who has to face the challenge, the great challenge. And very few people have chosen to risk, to go to the heights, to discover their ultimate peaks. Only a few—the Buddha, the Christ—only very few; they can be counted on the fingers.

Why hasn't the whole of humanity chosen to reach the same

state of bliss as Buddha, the same state of love as Christ, the same state of celebration as Krishna? Why? For the simple reason that it is dangerous even to aspire to those heights; it is better not to think about it. And the best way not to think about it is to accept that there is no freedom—you are already determined beforehand; there is a certain script handed over to you before your birth and you have just to fulfill it.

You ask: *"How can freedom be misused?"*

Only freedom can be misused; slavery cannot be misused. That's why you see so much chaos in the world today. It has never been there before, for the simple reason that man was not so free. You see more chaos in America than in Russia for the simple reason that in Russia people are not free to choose. In America, they are enjoying the greatest freedom that has ever been enjoyed anywhere in the world at any time in history. Whenever there is freedom, chaos erupts, but that chaos is worth it because only out of that chaos are stars born.

My people will be hated all over the world, will be condemned all over the world, for the simple reason that they have chosen to live a life of freedom. And I am not giving you any discipline, because every discipline is a subtle kind of slavery. I am not giving you any commandments, because any commandments given by anybody else coming from the outside are going to imprison you, to enslave you.

I am only teaching you how to be free and then leaving you to yourself to do what you want to do with your freedom. If you want to fall below the animals, that is your decision and you are perfectly allowed to do it, because it is your life. If you decide it that way, then it is your prerogative. But if you understand freedom and its value, you will not start falling, you will not go below the animals, you will start rising above the angels.

Man is not an entity, he is a bridge—a bridge between two eternities: the animal and the divine, the unconscious and the conscious. Grow in consciousness, grow in freedom, take each step out of your own choice: create yourself. A *sannyasin* is one who creates himself and takes the whole responsibility for it.

For a long time, I was desperately seeking spiritual truth. Despite what I felt to be many genuine spiritual experiences, I remained discontented and desperate. Lately, my burning desires for spiritual experience and the fruits of those experiences have been slowly disappearing. Nowadays I simply enjoy everyday life, and everything that goes with it—a tasty meal, a walk in the countryside, a good laugh with a loved one, and so on. Am I getting lazy on the way to enlightenment?

Can you please talk about the difference between falling asleep and letting go?

You are doing perfectly well. Just forget all about enlightenment. Enjoy simple things with total intensity. Just a cup of tea can be a deep meditation. If you can enjoy it, the aroma of it, slowly sipping it, the taste of it . . . who cares about God? You don't know that God is constantly feeling jealous of you when he sees you drinking a cup of tea, and the poor fellow cannot have it. Or instant coffee . . . these things are not available in the Garden of Eden. And since Adam and Eve left, there is no human company at all. God is just living with animals, who don't know how to make tea. God is jealous of you, and very repentant that he drove Adam and Eve out of the Garden of Eden, but now nothing can be done about it. The sons and daughters of Adam and Eve are living far more beautifully, far more richly.

Enlightenment happens when you have forgotten all about it. Don't look even out of the corner of your eye, just in case enlightenment is coming and you might miss it. Forget all about it. You just enjoy your simple life. And everything is so beautiful—why create unnecessary anxiety and anguish for yourself? Strange problems of spirituality . . . those things are not things you can do anything about.

If you can make your ordinary life a thing of beauty and art, all that you had always desired will start happening of its own accord.

There is a beautiful story. . . .

There is a temple in the state of Maharashtra in India. It is a temple devoted to Krishna, and a strange story is connected with it. In that temple, the statue of Krishna—in Maharashtra he is called Bitthal—is standing on a brick. Strange, because nowhere in any other temple is any of the gods standing on a brick.

The story is that one beautiful man, enjoying life every bit in its totality, was so contented and so fulfilled that Krishna decided to appear before him. Ordinarily there are people who are singing and dancing for their whole life, "Hare Krishna, Hare Rama," and neither Rama nor Krishna appears; nobody appears. This man was not bothering about Krishna or Rama or anybody. He was simply living his life, but living it the way it should be lived, with love, with heart, with beauty, with music, with poetry. His life was in itself a blessing, and Krishna decided, "This man needs a visit from me."

You can see the story—the man is not at all thinking of Krishna, but Krishna, on his own part, feels that this man deserves a visit. He goes in the middle of the night, not to create any trouble in the rest of the town. He finds the door open and he goes in.

The man's mother is very sick, and he is massaging her feet. Krishna comes behind him and says, "I am Krishna and I have come to give you an audience, a *darshana.*"

The man says, "This is not the right time; I am massaging my mother's feet." Meanwhile, just by his side there was a brick. He shoved the brick across the floor behind him—he did not even look to see who this Krishna was—and told him to sit down on it, and that when he was finished with his work he would see him. But he was so much absorbed in massaging the mother's feet—she was almost dying—that the whole night passed, with Krishna just sitting there. He said, "This is strange. People are singing their whole life long, 'Hare Krishna, Hare Rama' and I never go there. I have come here, and this fool has not even looked at me!" And then it was getting light, the sun was rising, and Krishna became worried because people would be passing by. The road was just by the side of the house, and the door was open, and if people saw him, soon there would be trouble; great crowds would come. So he disappeared, leaving just a stone statue of himself on the brick.

When the mother finally went to sleep, the man turned and said, "Who is the fellow who was disturbing me in the night?" And he found just a statue of Krishna. The whole village gathered—this was a miracle, what had happened? He told the whole story. They said, "You are a strange fellow. Krishna himself had come, but you are such a fool! You could have at least told him to sit down, offered him something to eat, something to drink. He was a guest."

The man said, "At that time, there was nothing by my side except this brick. And whenever I am doing something, I do it with totality. I don't want any interference. If he is so interested in being seen, he can come again; there is no hurry."

That statue remains in the temple of Bitthal, still standing on a brick. But the man was really a great man—not bothering about rewards or anything, absorbed so fully in every action that the action itself was the reward. Even if God comes, the reward coming out of the totality of action is greater than God.

Nobody has interpreted the story the way I am interpreting it, but you can see that any other interpretation is nonsense. So just forget about spirituality, enlightenment, God; they will take care of themselves, that is their business. They are just sitting there without customers. You need not worry; you do the best you can do with life. That is your test, that is your worship, that is your religion. Everything else will follow of its own accord.

Is sitting silently, doing nothing, watching the grass grow—and maybe falling asleep—really enough?

I once heard you say that we create our own lives, our own hells and miseries, and that we are responsible. If sitting silently really is enough, where does "effort" or "discipline" come in? Then, if we are doing something, what are we "doing"? Can we do anything at all, or am I just dreaming that I am doing something? Somewhere I am so tired of it. But then am I going to end up in a state of lethargy and indifference, in which I cannot see any love or beauty?

The people who have been exploiting humanity have created great philosophies, theologies, disciplines. Without the support of all this philosophical, theological, religious framework, it would be impossible to create the false personality. The word *discipline* comes from these people, and the word *effort* also comes from these people.

They have created such a world of emphasizing work, effort, endeavor, struggle, achievement, that they have turned almost everybody into workaholics—which is worse than being an alcoholic, because the alcoholic at least feels that he is doing something wrong. The workaholic feels he is doing the right thing, and those who are not workaholics are lazy people, worthless; they don't have any right even to exist, because they are a burden.

These people have destroyed beautiful words, given them new connotations, new meanings. For example, *discipline*. Discipline does not mean what you have heard it means. The word *discipline* comes from the same root as *disciple*. Its root meaning is: "the capacity to learn"; learning to be more sensitive, to be more aware, to be more sincere, to be more authentic, to be more creative. Life is a beautiful journey if it is a process of constant learning, exploration. Then it is excitement every moment, because every moment you are opening a new door, every moment you are coming in contact with a new mystery. The word *disciple* means "one who learns," and *discipline* means "the process of learning."

But the word has been prostituted, so that *discipline* means "obedience." They have turned the whole world into a camp of Boy Scouts! High above, there is somebody who knows—so you need not learn, you simply have to obey. They have turned the meaning of discipline into its very opposite.

Learning automatically consists of doubting, of questioning, of being skeptical, of being curious—not of being a believer, certainly, because a believer never learns. But they have used the word for thousands of years in this way. And it is not only one word that they have prostituted; they have prostituted many words. Beautiful words have become so ugly in the hands of the vested interests that you cannot even imagine the original meaning of the word. Thousands of years of misuse . . .

They want everybody to be disciplined the way people are disciplined in the army. You are ordered and you have to do it without asking why. This is not the way of learning.

Even from the very beginning, they have imposed stories on the minds of people, that the first sin committed was disobedience. Adam and Eve were expelled from the Garden of Eden because they disobeyed. I have tried in thousands of ways, but I don't see that they committed any sin or any crime. They were simply exploring! You are in a garden and you start exploring the fruits and flowers, and what is edible and what is not edible.

And God is responsible, because he prohibited them from two trees; he indicated the trees and said, "You should not approach these two trees. One is the tree of wisdom, and the other is the tree of eternal life." Just think, if you were Adam and Eve—was not God himself tempting you to go to these two trees? And those two trees were of wisdom and of eternal life. Why should God be against them? If he were really a father, one who loves you, he might have pointed to them, saying, "This is a poisonous tree, don't eat from it." Or, "This is the tree of death; if you eat anything, you will die. But these two trees are perfectly good! Eat as much as you can, because to be wise and to have eternal life is absolutely right."

Every father would wish his children to have wisdom and eternal life; this father seems to be absolutely loveless. Not only loveless, but as the devil said to Eve, "He has prevented you from these two trees. Do you know the reason? The reason is that if you eat from these two trees, you will be equal to him, and he is jealous. He does not want you to become divine. He does not want you to become gods, full of wisdom and eternal life."

I cannot see that the devil's argument has any flaw in it. It is absolutely right. In fact, he is the first benefactor of humanity. Without him, perhaps there would have been no humanity—no Gautam Buddha, no Kabir, no Christ, no Zarathustra, no Lao Tzu . . . just buffaloes, donkeys, yankees, all chewing grass contentedly. And God would have been very happy that his children were so obedient. But this obedience is poison, pure poison.

The devil must be counted as the first revolutionary of the world, and the first man to think in terms of evolution, of wisdom, of eternal life. And God said, or so the priests have been saying, the rabbis, Christian priests, Mohammedan *maulavis*, ayatollahs . . . they have been saying for centuries that it was the original sin. Again, another prostitution of a beautiful word. The word *sin* in its roots means "forgetfulness." It has nothing to do with sin as we have come to understand it. To forget yourself is the only sin, and to remember yourself is the only virtue. It has nothing to do with obedience, nothing to do with discipline.

The people who want to exploit... their very effort is that of a parasite, taking every drop of blood out of you. They say, "Work. Work hard, be disciplined, obey the orders. There is no need to question, because the orders are coming from a higher intelligence than you have." They are in such a mind that they don't even want you to sleep. In some places, they are developing a whole educational system: Every child will be educated during the day in school, but they say, "Why waste the whole night?" People after a while have to come out of the university and work in the world. But they work only a few hours, and their whole night is sheer waste; it can be used. So they are developing methods and means to use it. For example, it can be used for teaching. The child's ears could be hooked up to a subtle mechanism controlled by a central system in the town, and what they call "subliminal education" can be transmitted. It does not disturb your sleep—very softly, so quietly that it cannot even be called whispering, because even whispering may disturb your sleep... its range is lower than a whisper.

And about women, it has been known for centuries that if you want them to hear what you are saying, whisper. If you just start whispering with someone, any woman around is going to hear exactly what you are saying! If you are talking loudly, nobody cares. Whispering means that you are trying to hide, something is a secret. The woman, with her more sensitive being, becomes alert and she catches everything you are saying. So if you want to say anything to any woman, just whisper it to somebody else and she will get the message absolutely correctly!

The subliminal education experiments use a lower range of sound than whispering. They have found that it does not disturb sleep—it does not even disturb dreams. Dreams are at a certain level, sleep is at a deeper level than dreams, and subliminal whispering is deeper than sleep—so it simply goes on underground. For eight hours in the night you can teach whatever you want to teach, and the most wonderful thing about it is that the child will remember everything. There is no need to memorize it; there is no need to do homework for it. It has simply entered into the child's memory system from an underground source. Now they have captured your twenty-four hours! Even the freedom to dream may be taken away one day. It is possible that the government could decide what people should dream and what they should not dream. Dreams could be projected just like projecting pictures on a screen, and you would not be able to tell the difference, whether you are dreaming or the government agency is projecting some idea. Subliminal teaching is really one of the most dangerous things discovered by the researchers. It has been tried in many countries and found to work immensely well.

For example, you go into a movie and you see advertisements— they work, but they need constant repetition. A certain brand of cigarette . . . you have to see it in the newspaper, you have to see it on television, you have to hear it on the radio, you have to see it on the street on the billboards, you have to see it in the movie house; it has to be repeated continually. A certain brand . . . you don't take any note of it. You simply read it and you forget about it, but it is going to make a mark inside you. And when you go to purchase cigarettes, suddenly you will find yourself asking for that brand. But it is a long process. Up to now, advertising has been a lengthy process. Subliminal teaching would be a shortcut, and very dangerous. They have tried in a few movies, experimentally, to show the advertising between two frames. You are watching the movie and you will not be aware that something has happened; you will go on watching the movie. The story is going on, and in just a flash—so short that you will not be able to detect with your eyes that something has passed on the screen—you feel very thirsty and you need a Coca-Cola. You have not read Coca-Cola, but even though you have not read it, your memory has simply got the idea. And they have found that on the night of these experiments, in those particular movie houses, the sales of Coca-Cola could rise by 70 percent. The people who ask for Coca-Cola don't know why they are asking for Coca-Cola; they just feel thirsty. In reality, they are not feeling thirsty, they don't need Coca-Cola, but a subliminal impact has been made.

This is dangerous. It is taking away your freedom. You are not even free to choose, you are simply being ordered—and in such a way that you are not even aware that you have been ordered to purchase Coca-Cola.

Political parties are going to use it—"Vote for Ronald Reagan." There is no need to destroy all the walls and write everywhere, VOTE FOR RONALD REAGAN—just subliminal messages on television, in the movies.

Some educationalists are thinking that everybody's night can be used for further training, refresher courses. For example, a doctor comes out of the university, but medical science goes on growing and the doctor is always lagging far behind. He uses medicines that are no longer valid; science has gone ahead and has found better medicines. The doctor has no opportunity to read all that literature, but his night can be used. During the day he can look after the patients, and at night he can be given the latest information. But that means you have made the person a robot, twenty-four hours a day geared to work, and to do whatever kind of work you want. It is not the person's free will.

These types of people have brought these beautiful words like *discipline, work, obedience* to such a distasteful state that it is better for a few days to abandon them completely. Work is beautiful if it comes out of your love, if it comes out of your creativity. Then work has some spiritual quality. Discipline is good if it comes out of your learning, your disciplehood, your dedication, your devotion—then it is something that is growing in you like a beautiful flame, directing your life with its light. If obedience comes out of trust, then it is beautiful—not that somebody is more powerful and if you don't listen, you will be punished.

Even God could not forgive just one act of disobedience. The poor fellows . . . Adam and Eve had eaten one apple!

For five years, I lived mostly on apples. My mother used to say, "You should think about it—just one apple and Adam and Eve were turned out of the Garden of Eden. And you are simply living on apples!" For five years, I barely ate anything else. I said, "That's what I want to see . . . where will God send me? Now at the most he can drive me *into* the Garden of Eden. There are only two places, the Garden of Eden and the world. There is no other world he can drive me to." Naturally, God remained silent. "What to do now? This boy is committing sin from morning to night, sin upon sin"—because that was almost my only food.

God could not forgive a small thing. No, it is not the question that Adam and Eve had committed a great sin. The point is that

God's ego is hurt; it is a form of revenge. With great vengeance he punished them. It is unbelievable that even now you are suffering because of the sin committed by Adam and Eve. We don't know these people, when they existed, whether they existed or not; we have no part in their act; still, we are suffering?

Every human child is going to suffer such vengeance? It doesn't seem to be divine. God seems to be more evil than the devil. The devil seems to be more friendly, more understanding. The people who have poisoned these words—*work, discipline, obedience*—are the priests of this God. They represent him. They have destroyed the beauty of simple words.

Obedience can also be of tremendous beauty. But it should come out of your commitment, not out of an order from somebody. It should come out of your heart.

You love and you respect and you are dedicated to someone so deeply that your heart always says yes; it has forgotten how to say no. Even if you want to say no, you have forgotten the word. Then, obedience is religious, spiritual.

Is there another way without death and insecurity?

There is no death in the first place.

Death is an illusion.

It is always somebody else who dies; you never die. It means death has always been seen from the outside; it is the outsider's view.

Those who have seen their inner world are unanimous in saying that there is no death. Because you don't know what constitutes your consciousness; it is not constituted of breathing, it is not constituted of heartbeats, it is not constituted of blood circulation. So when the doctor says that a man is dead, it is an outsider's conclusion; all that he is saying is, "This man is no longer breathing, his pulse has stopped, his heart is not beating." Are these three things equivalent to death? They are not.

Consciousness is not your body, or your mind, or your heart.

So when a person dies, he dies for you, not for himself. For himself he simply changes the house, perhaps moves into a better apartment. But because the old apartment is left, and you are searching for him in the old apartment and you don't find him there, you think the poor guy is dead. All that you should say is, "The poor guy escaped. Now where he has gone, we don't know."

In fact, medical science is going beyond its limits when it says that some person is dead. Medical science has no right yet, because it has no definition yet of what constitutes death. It can simply say that "This man is no longer breathing. His heart has stopped. His pulse is no longer functioning." To conclude that he is dead is going beyond what you are seeing. But because science does not have any idea of consciousness, the death of the body becomes the death of the being.

Those who have known the being . . . and it is not necessary for it that you should die and then you know; you can just go inside. That's what I call meditation—just go inside and find out what is your center, and at your center there is no breathing, there is no heartbeat, there is no thought, no mind, no heart, no body, and still you are.

Once a person has experienced himself—that he is not the body, not the mind, not the heart, but pure awareness—he knows there is no death for him, because he does not depend on the body.

Awareness has no dependence on blood circulation. It does not depend on whether the heart beats or not, it does not depend on whether the mind functions or not. It is a totally different world; it is not constituted of any material thing, it is immaterial.

So the first thing to understand is that there is no death—it has never been found.

And if there is no death, what insecurity can there be?

For an immortal life, there can be no insecurity. Your immortality is not dependent on your bank balance; the beggar is as immortal as the emperor.

As far as people's consciousnesses are concerned, that is the only world where true communism exists: they all have equal qualities, and they don't have anything that can be lost or taken away. They don't have anything that can be destroyed, burned.

There is no insecurity.

All insecurity is a shadow of death.

If you look deeply, then every insecure feeling is rooted in the fear of death. But I am saying to you that there is no death; hence there cannot be any insecurity. You are immortal beings, *amritasya putrah*.

That's what the seers in the ancient East have said: You are the sons of immortality.

And they were not misers like Jesus Christ, that "I am the only begotten son of God." A strange idea . . . even to say it, one should feel ashamed. "I am the only begotten son of God" . . . What about others? Are they all bastards? Jesus is condemning the whole world! He is the son of God, and whose sons and daughters are all these people? And it is strange—why should God stop by giving birth to only one child? Is he spent just with one child? Or was he a believer in birth control?

I have been asking the pope and Mother Teresa, "Your God must be a believer in birth control, must be using things that you are prohibiting to people—condoms and all; otherwise, how is it possible? Once he created a son, then at least one daughter—that's a natural tendency."

And in the whole eternity . . . having no fun.

The psychologists say that poor people create more children for the simple reason that they don't have any other fun. To go to the cinema, you need money; to go to the circus, you need money; to go to Chowpatty Beach, you need money. Wherever there is fun, you need money. So just go to bed—that is the only fun without money, nobody asks for money.

What is God doing? Neither can he go to Chowpatty nor can he go to a circus nor to a cinema hall. Sitting eternally bored . . . . Just created one son? It has many implications: perhaps he was so frustrated with this one son that he became a celibate—"I am not going to create any more idiots."

Jesus was teaching on the earth for just three years. His age was only thirty-three, and he was crucified—a great savior who could not save himself. God must have felt tremendously let down: "Be finished! No more sons, no more daughters."

But the reality is that there is a certain element of egoism in being the only one, with no competitors.

Krishna may be the incarnation of God, but he is not the son—just a photocopy.

Mohammed may be a messenger—just a postman.

But Jesus is special; he is the only begotten son of God. There is a certain egoism in it.

The ancient seers were not so egoistic. They called the whole humanity—past, present, future—*amritasya putrah*: You are all sons of immortality. They are not putting themselves higher than you; they are not pretending to be holier than you. They are making every human being, as far as consciousness is concerned, absolutely equal, eternal.

There is no insecurity.

There is no need for any other path—and anyway, there is no other path.

Life is the path that passes through the illusory gate of death.

You can pass the gate consciously. If you are meditative enough, then you can go through death knowing perfectly that you are changing the house; you can enter another womb knowing perfectly that you are entering the new apartment—and it is always better, because life is always evolving. And if you can die consciously, then certainly your new life will be on a very high level, from the very beginning.

And I don't see any insecurity.

You come into the world without anything, so one thing is certain: Nothing belongs to you.

You come absolutely naked, but with illusions. That's why every child is born with closed hands, fists, believing that he is bringing treasures—and those fists are just empty. And everybody dies with open hands. Try to die with fists—nobody has been successful up to now. Or try to be born with open hands—nobody has been successful in that either.

The child is born with fists, with illusions that he is bringing treasures into the world, but there is nothing in the fist. Nothing belongs to you, so what insecurity? Nothing can be stolen; nothing can be taken away from you.

Everything that you are using belongs to the world.

And one day, you have to leave everything here.

You will not be able to take anything with you.

I have heard about a rich man in a village who was such a miser that he had never given anything to any beggar. The whole community of beggars knew about it, so whenever they saw some beggar standing before his house, they knew—"This man seems to be new, from some other village. Tell him, 'You won't get anything from there.'"

The man's wife was dying, but he wouldn't call the doctor. He had one friend only, because to have many friends means unnecessary insecurity—somebody may ask for money, somebody may ask for something. He had only one friend, and that one was also such a miser that there was no problem between them. They both understood each other's psychology—no conflict, no asking, no question of creating any embarrassment.

The friend said, "But this is the time that the doctor should be called—your wife is dying."

The man said, "It is all in the hands of God. What can a doctor do? If she is going to die, she is going to die. You will unnecessarily put me in trouble . . . paying the fee to the doctor for the medicine, this and that. I am a religious man, and if she is not going to die, she will recover without any doctor. The real doctor is God, nobody else. And I believe in God because he never asks for a fee or anything."

The wife died.

His friend said, "Look, just for a little money, you didn't call a doctor."

He said, "Little money? Money is money; it is never a question of a little. And death comes to everybody."

The friend was a little angry. He said, "This is too much. I am also a miser, but if my wife is dying, at least I will call a pharmacist—but I will call somebody. But you are really hard. What are you going to do with all this money?"

He said, "I am going to take it with me."

The friend said, "Nobody has ever heard of it."

He said, "But nobody has ever tried." That, too, was true. He said, "Just see. I have my own plan—I will take everything with me."

The friend said, "Just tell me your secret, because some day I will have to die also, and you are such a friend."

He said, "Friendship is one thing, but this secret I cannot tell. And the secret is such that you cannot use it when you are dying—it has to be used before, because you have to carry all your money and all your gold and diamonds and everything to the river."

He said, "What do you mean?"

He said, "Yes, and go into a small boat in the middle of the river and jump with all your money and be drowned—so you have taken it. Try! Nobody has tried. If you don't succeed, there is no harm, because everybody goes without it. If you succeed, then you will be the pioneer, the first one who reaches paradise with his whole bag of money. And all those saints will be looking with wide-open eyes—'This man has done something!'"

But the friend said, "That means you have to die."

He said, "Naturally, and you have to be in good health. When you are dying, then it will be very difficult to carry that heavy load. I am going to do it soon, because my wife is gone, now nobody is there."

But even if you jump in the ocean with all your money, the money will remain in the ocean, your body will remain in the ocean.

You will have to go alone, alone just as consciousness.

Nothing belongs to you, because you bring nothing here and you can take nothing from here.

Life is the only way.

Death is the only illusion to be understood.

If you can live fully, totally, understanding death as an illusion—not because I am saying it, but by your own experience in deep meditation—then live life fully, as totally as possible, without any fear. There is no insecurity, because even death is illusory.

Only the living being in you is real.

Clean it, sharpen it, make it fully aware so that not even a small part of it is drowned in darkness, so that you are luminous all over, you become aflame.

This is the only way; there is no other alternative.

And there is no need.

I am confused about the difference between individuality and personality. What, if anything, is left of the individual after the exit of the ego?

Individuality is your essence. You come with it; you are born with it. Personality is borrowed. It is given by the society to you. It is just like clothes, subtle clothes.

A child is born naked; then we hide his nakedness—we give him clothes. A child is born with essence, individuality. We hide that, too, because naked individuality is rebellious, nonconformist.

Individuality is exactly what it means. It is individual. Personality is not individual; it is social. Society wants you to have personalities, not individualities, because your individualities will create conflict. The society hides your individuality and gives a personality.

Personality is a learned thing. The word *personality* comes from a Greek root that means "mask"—*persona*. In Greek drama, the actors used to wear masks to hide their real faces and to show some other face. From *persona* comes the word *personality*. It is a face that you wear; it is not your original face.

When the personality disappears, don't be afraid. Then for the first time you become authentic. For the first time you become real. For the first time you attain to essence. That essence in India has been called *atman*, the soul.

The ego is the center of personality, and the divine is the center of essence. That's why so much insistence, from every corner, that the ego has to be dropped. Because you must know what you are, not what you are expected to be.

Personality is false; it is the greatest lie. The whole society depends on personality. The state, the church, the organizations, the establishments—they are all lies. Western psychology goes on thinking too much about the personality. That's why the whole of Western psychology is a psychology based on a basic lie.

In the East, we think of the essence, not of the personality. That which you have brought, that which is your intrinsic nature, *swabhava*, that which is your intrinsic essence—that has to be known, and that has to be lived.

Personality is that which you are not, but try to show that you are. Personality is that which, when you move in society, you have to use as a convenience.

You are walking, you have gone for a morning walk and somebody passes by. You smile. The smile can be either from the essence or from the personality. The smile can really be a delight in seeing the person, in seeing the godliness in that person, in seeing the heart, the love, the formless, that has become incarnate in that person.

That's why in India we never use phrases like *good morning*. They don't mean much. We say *Ram, Ram. . . .* We welcome each other by the name of God. It is a symbolic act: "I see God within you. Welcome. I am happy, blessed, that you passed." If it comes from the essence, then the smile spreads all over your being. You feel a deep content. You feel blessed that this person passed by. The person may be gone, but the blessing remains and lingers around you like a subtle perfume.

But you can simply say good morning—because the man is a banker, or a political leader, or can be sometimes mischievous, or can be dangerous and it is risky not to say good morning. Then you say it and you smile; you bring a smile to your face. That is *persona*; that is personality.

In each act you have to watch. It is arduous, but it has to be done. There is no other way. In each act you have to watch from where it comes. From personality or from essence?

If it comes from essence, the essence will grow, because you will give an opportunity for the essence to be manifested, expressed. If it comes from the personality, then personality will become harder and harder and harder, and it will suffocate the essence completely.

Watch. Remind yourself again and again to watch: "From where does it come?"

If you come home and you bring ice cream, flowers to your wife, is the present from the personality or from the essence? If it is from the personality, it is a lie. You may have talked to somebody else's wife, and you were charmed. You felt attracted, a desire arose in you and then you started feeling guilty: "This is not faithfulness. So take some ice cream home."

And remember—your wife will immediately suspect! Otherwise, you never bring ice cream. There must be something in it; you must be hiding something. Why are you so good today, so suddenly, unexpectedly good? You cannot deceive women; they have an instinct, they are lie detectors. They immediately feel first; they don't think. Their feeling is immediate and direct. They function from the center of emotion. You are feeling guilty; then you bring some presents to the wife. It is a gift from the personality. It is very dangerous!

A similar but opposite case can happen. The situation may be the same. You were talking to your friend's wife. You were charmed. She was graceful and beautiful, and because of her beauty, because of her grace, you remembered your wife. Because when you love a person every other beautiful person reminds you of the person. It has to be so. If the woman was charming, it immediately reminds you of your beloved. Something of the beloved was there—a part, a gesture. Something of your wife was there. You loved the woman in that moment because she reminded you of your wife. Then you are full of the memory.

Then you may bring ice cream or flowers or something . . . or nothing, just a smile. Then it is from the essence; then it is totally different. The situation may be the same, but you can behave in a totally different way.

Personality is an effort to deceive. Essence is an effort to reveal your being; whatsoever it is—it is. Let it be revealed, and be open, and be vulnerable.

Try to live from the essence, and you will become religious. Try to live by the personality, and you will be the most irreligious possible.

To me, religion doesn't mean a ritual. It doesn't mean going to the church or the temple. It doesn't mean reading the Bible or the Gita every day, no. Religion means to live from the essence, to be authentic, to be true.

And remember, in whatever way you lie, you cannot get away with a lie, because a lie is a lie. Deep down, you know it is a lie. You may pretend that you don't know, but your pretension will be there and that will indicate it. You cannot really lie to anybody, because anybody who has any eyes, who has any awareness, any intelligence will penetrate into it.

There was a case. A woman was suing Mulla Nasruddin. She claimed that her child was Mulla Nasruddin's child. And Mulla was denying it vehemently in the court.

Finally, the judge asked: "Say only one thing—did you sleep with this woman, Nasruddin?"

Nasruddin said: "No, Your Honor—not a wink."

Your lies are apparent, because the truth has a way of coming up. It finds a way. In the end, the truth is known, and you wasted your whole life in lies.

Don't waste a single moment. All the time that is wasted in lies is absolutely wasted. And through lies, nobody ever becomes happy; it is impossible. Lies can give only pretensions of happiness; they cannot give you true happiness.

True happiness is part of truth. Hindus have defined God as bliss—*satchitanand*, truth, consciousness, bliss. *Anand*, bliss, is the final, the ultimate core.

Be true, and you will be blissful. Be authentic, and you will be happy. And that happiness will be uncaused; it will be just a part of your being true. Happiness is a function of truth. Whenever there is truth, happiness functions. Whenever there is not truth, happiness stops functioning and unhappiness functions.

Don't be afraid. You say: *"I am confused about the difference between individuality and personality. What, if anything, is left of the individual after the exit of the ego?"*

In fact, because of the ego, nothing of the individual is left. When the ego is gone, the whole individuality arises in its crystal purity: transparent, intelligent, radiant, happy, alive, vibrating with an unknown rhythm. That unknown rhythm is divine. It is a song heard in the deepest core of your being. It is a dance of the formless. But one can hear the footsteps.

Everything real arises only when the ego has gone. Ego is the deceiver, the falsification. When ego is gone, *you* are there. When ego is there, you simply think you are, but you are not.

How do I become integrated?

Integration has nothing to do with becoming. In fact, all efforts to become bring *dis*integration. Integration is already there at the deepest core of your being; it has not to be brought in.

At your very center you are integrated; otherwise you could not exist at all. How can you exist without a center? The bullock-cart moves, the wheel moves, because there is an unmoving center on which the wheel moves. It moves on the hub. If the cart is moving, the hub is there. You may know it; you may not know it.

You are alive, you are breathing, you are conscious; life is moving, so there must be a hub to the wheel of life. You may not be aware, but it is there. Without it, you cannot be.

So the first thing, and very fundamental: Becoming is not the issue. You are. You have just to go in and see it. It is a discovery, not an achievement. You have been carrying it all along. But you have become too attached to the periphery, and your back is to the center. You have become too outgoing, so you cannot look in.

Create a little insight. The word *insight* is beautiful—it means "sight in," to look in, to see in. Eyes open outward, hands spread outward, legs move away from you. Sit silently, relax the periphery, close your eyes, and just go in . . . and not with effort. Just relax—as if one is drowning and one cannot do anything. We go on doing even when we are drowning.

If you can simply allow it to happen, it will come to the surface. Out of the clouds, you will see the center arising.

There are two modes of life. One is the action mode—you do something. The other is the reception mode—you simply receive. The action mode is outgoing. If you want more money, you cannot just sit. It is not going to come that way. You will have to struggle for it, compete, and you will have to use all sorts of ways and means—legal, illegal, right, wrong. Money is not going to come by just sitting. If you want to become powerful, if you want to become a politician, you will have to do something about it. It is not going to come on its own.

There is an action mode. The action mode is the outgoing mode. And there is an inaction mode, too: you don't do anything; you simply allow it to happen. We have forgotten that language. That forgotten language has to be learned again.

Integration has not to be brought in—it is already there. We have forgotten how to look at it; we have forgotten how to understand it. Move from the action mode more and more to the receptive, passive mode.

I'm not saying to leave the world of action—because that will make you lopsided again. You are lopsided right now. You have only one mode to your life, and that is action, doing something. There are people who cannot imagine sitting silently; it is impossible. They cannot allow themselves a moment's relaxation. They are interested only in action.

I have heard. . .

Mulla Nasruddin's wife was standing near the window, and it was a beautiful sunset, and the birds were flying back to their nests. It was really a wonderful evening. And she told Nasruddin, "Look! Come here. See what a beautiful sunset!"

Nasruddin, without even looking up from his news-paper, said, "Now, what did you say he was doing, this sun?"

If something is being *done*, then he is interested. If it is just a sunset, then what is the point of looking at it?

You are interested only in action, interested only if "something is happening." This has become too fixed. This has to be relaxed a little; you have to go for a few moments, for a few hours, some-times for a few days, totally to the other mode of life, just sitting and allowing things to happen. When you look at a sunset, you are not expected to do anything. You simply look. When you look at a flower, what are you supposed to do? You simply look.

In fact, there is no effort, even of looking at the flower. It is effortless. Your eyes are open, the flower is there . . . a moment of deep communion comes when the looked-at and the looker both disappear. Then there is beauty; then there is benediction. Then suddenly you are not the observer, and the flower is not the observed—because to observe there must still be some action. Now you are there and the flower is there, and somehow you overlap each other's boundaries. The flower enters into you, you enter into the flower, and there is a sudden revelation. Call it beauty, call it truth, call it godliness. . . .

These rare moments have to be allowed more and more. I can-not say they have to be cultivated, I cannot say you have to train for those moments, I cannot say that you have to do something—because again that will be using the language of the action mode, and will be deeply misinterpreted. No, I can simply say to allow these moments more and more. Sometimes, simply don't do any-thing. Relax on the lawn and look at the sky. Sometimes close the eyes and just look at your inner world—thoughts moving, float-ing; desires arising, going. Look at the colorful dream world that goes on within you. Just look. Don't say, "I want to stop these thoughts"—again you have moved into the action mode. Don't say, "I am meditating—go! All thoughts, go away from me"— because if you start saying that, you have started doing something. No, be as if you are not.

There is one of the most ancient meditations still used in some monasteries of Tibet. The meditation is based on the truth that I am saying to you. They teach that sometimes you can simply dis-appear. Sitting in the garden, you just start feeling that you are disappearing. Just see how the world looks when you have gone from the world, when you are no longer here, when you have be-come absolutely transparent. Just try for a single second not to be.

In your own home, be as if you are not.

Just think: One day you will not be. One day you will be gone, you will be dead; the radio will still continue, the wife will still prepare the breakfast, the children will still be getting ready for school. Think: Today you are gone; you just are not. Become a ghost. Just sitting in your chair, you simply disappear, you simply think, "I have no more reality; I am not." And just see how the house continues. There will be tremendous peace and silence. Everything will continue as it is. Without you, everything will continue as it is. Nothing will be missed. Then what is the point of always remain-ing occupied, doing something, doing something, obsessed with action? What is the point? You will be gone, and whatever you have done will disappear—as if you had signed your name on the sands, and the wind comes and the signature disappears and ev-erything is finished. Be as if you had never existed.

It is really a beautiful meditation. You can try it many times in twenty-four hours. Just half a second will do; for half a second, simply stop . . . you are not . . . and the world continues. When you become more and more alert to the fact that without you, the world continues perfectly well, then you will be able to learn another part of your being that has been neglected for long, for lives—and that is the receptive mode. You simply allow; you become a door. Things go on happening without you.

Become a piece of driftwood. Float in the stream like timber, and wherever the stream goes, let it take you; you don't make any effort. The whole Buddhist approach belongs to the receptive mode. That's why you see Buddha sitting under a tree. All his images are of sitting, sitting and doing nothing. He's simply sitting there; he's not doing anything.

You don't have that type of image of Jesus. He still goes on following the action mode. That's where Christianity has missed the deepest possibility: Christianity became active. The Christian missionary goes on serving the poor, goes to the hospital, does this and that, and his whole effort is to do something good. Yes, very good—but he remains in the action mode, and the divine can be known only in the receptive mode. So a Christian missionary will be a good man, a very good man, but not, in the Eastern sense, a sage.

Now even in the East, a person who goes on doing things is worshipped as a mahatma—because the East is poor, ill. There are thousands of lepers, blind people, uneducated people; they need education, they need medicine, they need service, they need a thousand and one things. Suddenly the active person has become important—so Gandhi is a mahatma, Vinoba Bhave is a saint, Mother

Teresa of Calcutta has become very important. But nobody looks at whether they have attained to the receptive mode or not.

Now if Buddha comes, nobody is going to pay respect to him, because he will not be running a school or a hospital. He will again be sitting under a bodhi tree, just sitting silently. Not that nothing is done by him—tremendous vibes are created by his being, but they are very subtle. He transforms the whole world by sitting under his bodhi tree, but to recognize those vibrations, you will have to be attuned, you will have to grow.

To recognize a Buddha is to be already on the path. To recognize a Mother Teresa is very easy—there is nothing much in it. Anybody can see that she is doing good work.

To do good work is one thing, and to *be* good is totally another. I'm not saying don't do good works. I am saying, let good works come out of your *being* good.

First attain to the receptive mode, first attain to the passive, first attain to the nonactive. And when your inner being flowers and you have come to know the integration inside—which is always there, the center is always there—when you have recognized that center, suddenly death disappears for you. Suddenly all worries disappear because you are no more a body now, and no more a mind.

Then compassion arises, love arises, prayer arises. You become a showering, a blessing to the world. Now, nobody can say what will happen to such a man—whether he will go and become a revolutionary like Jesus and chase the moneylenders from the temple; or whether he will go and serve poor people; or whether he will just continue sitting under the bodhi tree and spreading his fragrance; or whether he will become a Meera and dance and sing the glory of God. Nobody knows; it is unpredictable.

You ask me, *"How to become integrated?"*

My whole effort here is to make you aware that nothing is needed, nothing more is needed. You have it already there, existing inside you. But you have to make approaches, doors, ways to discover it. You have to dig for it; the treasure is there.

So it is not a question of how to become integrated. "How to know that I am already integrated?" is the right question.

The question comes from Nisagar, and I can understand why it comes from her. She has been related to Gurdjieff work in the West. Gurdjieff had a very strange idea—meaningful, but still strange. He used to say to his disciples, "The soul does not exist. The center does not exist; it has to be created. Man is not born with a soul"...a very strange theory. But I can understand what he was emphasizing: Man is not born with a soul; he has to crystallize his soul by effort. Hence Gurdjieff's whole system is called "the work." It is work and work and work. It is effort—again the action mode.

In fact, in the West, it is very difficult to teach people the non-action mode. So Gurdjieff was teaching techniques, methods of how to become integrated. He would say, "There is no soul already there." Not that there is no soul, and not that he was not aware of it; but it was a device. People had become very lethargic about the soul. They thought it was already there, so why worry, why bother? "It is there. Any day we can find it, so let us in the meanwhile find other things that are not already there. Meanwhile, let us find beautiful women, more wine, more money, more power— things that are not there, let us seek these. And the day we are fed up with all this, at any moment, we will close our eyes and we will go in, and the soul will be there. It is never lost; you cannot lose it and you cannot gain it. It is already there." So people have become very lethargic.

You can see it in the East. The whole East has become so lousy and lethargic. The soul is there and everybody knows it, everybody has heard it. "God is within the heart, he is already there, so why create any fuss about him?" People seek that which is *not* there.

Gurdjieff became aware of this fact, that the idea that the soul is already there had made people very lethargic, uninterested in the soul—very uninterested, absolutely uninterested in the inner world. The mind is interested only in that which gives a challenge, which is an adventure. So Gurdjieff, to fit with the Western mind, started saying that the soul is *not* there: "Don't sit patiently, do something—because when people die, all of them don't survive. Only those who have integrated their centers will survive. Others will simply disappear like vegetables. So it is for you to choose. You are taking a risk," Gurdjieff said. "If you do something—and doing means arduous doing, hard work, a whole life devoted to it—then only will you be able to survive death. Otherwise you are going to be discarded. You will be thrown in the junkyard. The immortal is not going to choose you unless you are integrated. You have to earn it. Only very few will be saved after death, not all."

This was a strange theory, never propounded before, never in the whole history of humanity. There have been people who said, "There is no soul." We know them; they are atheists. They have always been there. There are people who say, "There is soul, and it cannot be destroyed. Even death cannot destroy it." We have heard about them; they have always been there. But Gurdjieff was saying something absolutely new, something that had never been said before. He was saying, "Soul is *possible;* it is not actual. It is simply possible. You may attain to it, you may not attain to it—you may miss it. There is more possibility that you will miss it, because the way you are living, you are not earning it."

Gurdjieff said, "Man is like a seed. It is not necessary that the seed will become a tree. It is not necessary—the seed may not find the right soil. Even if the right soil is found, there may be no rains. Or even if there are rains, animals may come and destroy the plant. There are a thousand and one difficulties. The seed is not going to necessarily be a tree. If one thousand and one protections are taken, only then will the seed become a tree. You are not a soul; you are just a possibility. A thousand and one efforts have to be made; only then will you become a soul. Only rarely: in one million, one person becomes a soul. All others simply vegetate, die, and disappear."

I say it is a strange theory, because it is not true. And I say it is very meaningful, because something like this is needed—at least in the West it is needed. Otherwise, nobody bothers about the soul. But all the techniques that Gurdjieff was using are basically the same techniques that we have used in the East for discovering the soul. He simply changed the words. He called it "creating the soul," integrating the soul, crystallizing the center. But those techniques are the same.

You are already integrated. Not on the periphery—on the periphery there is much turmoil. You are fragmented on the periphery. Move inward, and the deeper you go, the more you will find that you are integrated. There comes a point, at the very innermost shrine of your being, where you suddenly find you are a unity, absolute unity. So it is a question of discovering.

How to discover it?

I would like to give you a technique. It is a very simple technique, but in the beginning, it looks very hard. If you try, you will find it is simple. If you don't try and only think about it, it will look very hard. The technique is this: Do only that which you enjoy. If you don't enjoy it, don't do it. Try it—because enjoyment comes only from your center. If you are doing something and you enjoy it, you start getting reconnected with the center. If you do something you don't enjoy, you are disconnected from the center. Joy arises from the center, and from nowhere else. So let it be a criterion, and be a fanatic about it.

You are walking on the road; suddenly you recognize that you are not enjoying the walk. Stop. Finished—this is not to be done.

I used to do it in my university days, and people thought that I was crazy. Suddenly I would stop, and then I would remain in that spot for half an hour, an hour, unless I started enjoying walking again. My professors were so afraid that when there were examinations, they would put me in a car and take me to the university hall. They would leave me at the door and wait there: Had I reached my desk or not? If I was taking my bath and suddenly I realized that I was not enjoying it, I would stop. What is the point then? If I was eating and I recognized suddenly that I was not enjoying, then I would stop.

I had joined the mathematics class in my high school. The first day, I went in and the teacher was just introducing the subject. In the middle, I stood up and tried to walk out. He said, "Where are you going? Without asking, I won't allow you in again." I said, "I'm not coming back again; don't be worried. That's why I am not asking. Finished—I am not enjoying it! I will find some other subject I can enjoy, because if I cannot enjoy it, I am not going to do it. It is torture; it is violence."

And, by and by, it became a key. I suddenly recognized that whenever you are enjoying something, you are centered. Enjoyment is just the sound of being centered. Whenever you are not enjoying something, you are off center. Then don't force it; there is no need. If people think you crazy, let them think you crazy. Within a few days you will, by your own experience, find how you were missing yourself. You were doing a thousand and one things that you never enjoyed, and still you were doing them because you were taught to. You were just fulfilling your duties.

People have destroyed even such a beautiful thing as love. You come home and you kiss your wife because it has to be so, it has to be done. Now, a beautiful thing like a kiss, a flowerlike thing, has been destroyed. By and by, without enjoying it, you will go on kissing your wife; you will forget the joy of kissing another human being. You shake hands with anybody you meet—the handshake is cold, with no meaning in it, with no message in it, no warmth flowing. It is just dead hands shaking each other and saying hello. Then you start, by and by, learning this dead gesture, this cold gesture. You become frozen; you become an ice cube. And then you ask, "How to enter to the center?"

The center is available when you are warm, when you are flowing, melting, in love, in joy, in dance, in delight. It is up to you. Just go on doing only those things that you really love to do and you enjoy. If you don't enjoy, stop. Find something else that you will enjoy.

There is bound to be something that you will enjoy. I have never come across a person who cannot enjoy anything. There are persons who may not enjoy one thing, then another, then another, but life is vast. Don't remain engaged; become floating. Let there be more streaming of energy. Let it flow, let it meet with other energies that surround you. Soon you will be able to see that the problem was not how to become integrated; the problem was that you have forgotten how to flow. In a flowing energy, you are suddenly integrated. It happens sometimes accidentally, too, but the reason is the same.

Sometimes you fall in love with a woman or a man, and suddenly you feel integrated, suddenly you feel you are one for the first time. Your eyes have a glow, your face has a radiance, and your intellect is no longer dull. Something starts burning bright in your being; a song arises, your walk has a quality of dance in it now. You are a totally different being.

But these are rare moments, because we don't learn the secret. The secret is that there is something you have started to enjoy. That's the whole secret. A painter may be hungry and painting, and still you can see that his face is so contented. A poet may be poor, but when he is singing his song, he is the richest man in the world. Nobody is more rich than he is. What is the secret of it? The secret is, he is enjoying this moment. Whenever you enjoy something, you are in tune with yourself and you are in tune with the universe— because your center is the center of all.

So let this small insight be a climate for you: do only that which you enjoy, otherwise stop. You are reading a newspaper and halfway through it you suddenly recognize that you are not enjoying it: then there is no necessity. Then why are you reading? Stop it here and now. If you are talking to somebody and in the middle you recognize that you are not enjoying it, you have just said half a sentence, stop then and there. You are not enjoying; you are not obliged to continue. In the beginning, it will look a little weird.

But my people are weird, so I don't think there is any problem. You can practice it.

Within a few days, many contacts will be made with the center, and then you will understand what I mean when I go on repeating again and again that that which you are seeking is already in you. It is not in the future. It has nothing to do with the future. It is already here now, it is already the case.

Epilogue

A man came to Junnaid, a Sufi mystic, and asked him, "What do you say about predetermination, kismet, fate, and the freedom of man? Is man free to do whatever he wants to do? Or is he simply a puppet in the hands of an unknown puppeteer, who just dances the dance that the puppeteer chooses?"

Junnaid is one of the world's most beautiful mystics. He shouted at the man, "Raise up one leg!"

The questioner was a very rich man, and Junnaid knew that about him. All his disciples, the whole school knew about it—and Junnaid had shouted so loudly and so rudely, "Raise one leg up!" The rich man had never followed anybody's orders; he had not come to see Junnaid in order to follow orders, and he could not imagine even a far-fetched, off-the-wall relationship between his question and this answer. But when you are facing a man like Junnaid you have to follow him.

The man raised his right leg.

Junnaid said, "That is not enough. Now raise the other, too."

Now the man was at a loss, and angry also. He said, "You are asking absurdities! I had come to ask an important question—you simply dropped that question without answering, and you asked me to raise one leg. I raised my right leg. And now you are asking me to raise the other, too? What do you want? How can I raise both legs?"

Junnaid said, "Then sit down. Have you received the answer to your question or not?"

The man said, "The answer to my question has not been given yet. Instead you have been training me for some kind of weird parade!"

Junnaid said, "See the point: When I told you to raise one of your legs, you had the freedom to choose either the right or the left. Nobody was determining it; it was your choice to raise the right leg. But once you had chosen the right leg, you could not choose the left, too. It is your freedom that has determined the facts of your bondage. Now your left leg is in bondage."

Man is half free and half in bondage, but he is free first.

And it is his freedom, how he uses his freedom, that determines his bondage. There is nobody sitting there writing in your head or making lines on your palms. Even an omnipotent God would be tired by now, doing this stupid thing of making lines on people's hands. And so many people are always being born into the world—writing in everybody's head what he is going to be, where he is going to be born, when he is going to die, of what disease, or what doctor is going to kill him . . . all these details! Either God would have gone mad doing all this work—just think of yourself, if you had to do this kind of work, and for no reason—or he would have committed suicide. Even if he were mad, he would still have to do his work. So for a few days, he may have been mad, while he created this humanity, and then he must have committed suicide, because he would not want to see the world evaporate because of nuclear weapons. But he has written those nuclear weapons in your heads; he is responsible.

Nobody is responsible, and there is no God. These are our strategies to throw responsibility into others' hands.

You are free, but each act of freedom brings a responsibility—and that is your bondage. Either call it bondage, which is not a beautiful word, or call it responsibility. That is what I call it.

You choose a certain act—that is your freedom. But then the consequences will be your responsibility.

I am in absolute agreement with the idea of science that cause and effect are together. As far as the cause is concerned, you are free. But then you should remember: The effect is decided by you, by your cause. In fact, you are free in that, too; it is an outcome of your freedom.

Take life in a very simple, nontheological way, and you will be surprised: there are no problems.

It is a mystery, but not a problem.

A problem is that which can be solved; a mystery is that which can be lived but can never be solved. And meditation is nothing but an exploration of the mystery—not an explanation, not a search to find the solution to it, but an exploration. . . . To dissolve into it slowly, just as a ripple disappears into the ocean; this disappearance is the only religiousness that I know of. All else is nonsense.

About the Author

Osho's teachings defy categorization, covering everything from the individual quest for meaning to the most urgent social and political issues facing society today. His books are not written but are transcribed from audio and video recordings of extemporaneous talks given to international audiences over a period of thirty-five years. Osho has been described by the *Sunday Times* in London as one of the "1,000 Makers of the Twentieth Century" and by American author Tom Robbins as "the most dangerous man since Jesus Christ."

About his own work, Osho has said that he is helping to create the conditions for the birth of a new kind of human being. He has often characterized this new human being as "Zorba the Buddha"— capable both of enjoying the earthy pleasures of a Zorba the Greek and the silent serenity of a Gautam Buddha. Running like a thread through all aspects of Osho's work is a vision that encompasses both the timeless wisdom of the East and the highest potential of Western science and technology.

Osho is also known for his revolutionary contribution to the science of inner transformation, with an approach to meditation that acknowledges the accelerated pace of contemporary life. His unique "active meditations" are designed to first release the accumulated stresses of body and mind, so that it is easier to experience the thought-free and relaxed state of meditation.

Osho International Meditation Resort

The Osho International Meditation Resort is a place where people can have a direct personal experience of a new way of living with more alertness, relaxation, and fun. Located about one hundred miles southeast of Mumbai in Pune, India, the resort offers a variety of programs to thousands of people who visit each year from more than a hundred countries around the world.

Originally developed as a summer retreat for maharajas and wealthy British colonials, Pune is now a thriving modern city that is home to a number of universities and high-tech industries. The Meditation Resort spreads over forty acres in a tree-lined suburb known as Koregaon Park. The resort campus provides accommodations for a limited number of guests, and there is a plentiful variety of nearby hotels and private apartments available for stays of a few days up to several months.

Resort programs are all based in the Osho vision of a qualitatively new kind of human being who is able both to participate creatively in everyday life and to relax into silence and meditation. Most programs take place in modern air-conditioned facilities and include a variety of individual sessions, courses, and workshops covering everything from creative arts to holistic health treatments, personal transformation and therapy, esoteric sciences, the Zen approach to sports and recreation, relationship issues, and significant life transitions for men and women. Individual sessions and group workshops are offered throughout the year, alongside a full daily schedule of meditations.

Outdoor cafés and restaurants within the resort grounds serve both traditional Indian fare and a choice of international dishes, all made with organically grown vegetables from the resort's own farm. The campus has its own private supply of safe, filtered water.

See www.osho.com/resort for more information, including travel tips, course schedules, and guesthouse bookings.

For More Information

For further information about Osho and his work, see

www.osho.com

a comprehensive Web site in several languages that includes an online tour of the Meditation Resort and a calendar of its course offerings, a catalog of books and tapes, a list of Osho information centers worldwide, and selections from Osho's talks.

Or contact Osho International, e-mail: oshointernational@ oshointernational.com.

About the DVD

The enclosed Osho DVD contains one of the original talks by Osho, and has been chosen to give you a taste of the work of a contemporary mystic. Osho did not write his books: he rather speaks directly to people, creating an atmosphere and experience of meditation and transformation.

The video provides English language subtitles as an option.

The purpose of the Osho talks is not to provide information or entertainment—although they can be both informative and entertaining—but rather to provide an opportunity for meditation, to experience the state of relaxed alertness that lies at the core of meditation. With this understanding, it is suggested that a time be set aside for viewing the video for at least forty-five minutes to an hour without interruption.

Here is what Osho says about listening to his talks:

How to give people a taste of meditation was my basic reason to speak, so I can go on speaking eternally—it does not matter what I am saying. All that matters is that I give you a few chances to be silent, which you find difficult on your own in the beginning.

These discourses are the foundations of your meditation.

I am making you aware of silences without any effort on your part. My speaking is for the first time being used as a strategy to create silence in you.

I don't speak to teach something; I speak to create something. These are not lectures; these are simply a device for you to become silent, because if you are told to become silent without making any effort, you will find great difficulty.

I don't have any doctrine; my talking is really a process of dehypnosis. Just listening to me, slowly, slowly you will be free of all the programs that the society has forced you to believe in.

These questions and answers are really just a game to help you to get rid of words, thoughts. . . . Silence is the question. Silence is the answer. Silence is the ultimate truth.

In silence we meet with existence.

These are not ordinary discourses or talks. I am not interested in any philosophy or any political ideology. I am interested directly in transforming you.

OSHO

LOOK WITHIN...

BODY MIND BALANCING: USING YOUR MIND TO HEAL YOUR BODY

Developed by Osho, BODY MIND BALANCING is a relaxation and meditation process for reconnecting with your body, complete with a guided audio process. The guided meditation and relaxation process, "Reminding Yourself of the Forgotten Language of Talking to Your BodyMind" accompanies the text on CD.

ISBN: 0-312-33444-3 • Paperback w/CD
$15.95/$17.95 Can.

MEDITATION: THE FIRST AND LAST FREEDOM

A practical guide to integrating meditation into all aspects of daily life, which includes instructions for more than 60 meditation techniques, including the revolutionary Osho Active Meditations.™

ISBN: 0-312-33663-2 • Paperback • $13.95/$15.50 Can.

LIFE, LOVE, LAUGHTER:
CELEBRATING YOUR EXISTENCE

In this collection of reflections, Osho's inspiring and loving stories go far beyond the usual chicken-soup fare. Osho mixes entertainment and inspiration, ancient Zen stories and contemporary jokes to help us find love, laughter, and ultimately, happiness. An original talk by Osho on DVD is included

ISBN: 0-312-53109-5 • Paperback w/DVD
$14.95/$18.95 Can.

LOVE, FREEDOM, ALONENESS:
THE KOAN OF RELATIONSHIPS

Love can only happen through freedom and in conjunction with a deep respect for ourselves and the other. Is it possible to be alone and not lonely? Where are the boundaries that define "lust" versus "love" and can lust ever grow into love? Osho offers unique, radical, and intelligent perspectives on thes and other essential questions, as well as a golden opportunity to start afresh with ourselves, our relationships to others, and to find fulfillment and success for the individual and for society as a whole

ISBN: 0-312-29162-0 • Paperback • $15.99/$20.50 Can.

OSHO INSIGHTS FOR A NEW WAY OF LIVING SERIES

The Insights for a New Way of Living series aims to shine light on beliefs and attitudes that prevent individuals from being their true selves. Each book is an artful mixture of compassion and humor, and readers are encouraged to confront what they would most like to avoid, which in turn provides the key to true insight and power.

0-312-53857-X

0-312-20517-1

0-312-27563-3

0-312-27566-8

0-312-20519-8

0-312-36568-3

Please visit **www.stmartins.com/osho** for additional information on these titles, as well as *FREEDOM, INTELLIGENCE, INTUITION,* and *MATURITY.*

OSHO TAKE A NEW LOOK www.OSHO.com

 ST. MARTIN'S GRIFFIN